Eighty Precious Chinese Recipes

Eighty Precious Chinese Recipes

MAY WONG TRENT

Macmillan Publishing Co., Inc.
New York
Collier Macmillan Publishers
London

To my family, to Peter,
for sharing my love
for good food and good cooking

Copyright © 1973 by May Wong Trent

All rights reserved. No part of this book may be repro-
duced or transmitted in any form or by any means,
electronic or mechanical, including photocopying, re-
cording or by any information storage and retrieval system, without permission in writing from the publisher.
Macmillan Publishing Co., Inc.
Collier-Macmillan Canada Ltd.

Library of Congress Catalog Card Number: 72-92002

First Printing

Printed in the United States of America

Foreword

Hello! Welcome to Chinese cooking.

I hope you'll use this book often. I usually buy a cookbook when it contains a recipe that appeals to me so much I cannot wait to get home to try it. It is only then that I feel justified in buying a new cookbook.

In my cooking classes, I always urge my students to go right home and try the dish we have just cooked together in school—it helps make that dish part of the student's cooking repertoire and, like buying a new cookbook, it seems to make it all worth the effort and the expense.

Will you cook along with me, too?

You need Chinese ingredients to cook Chinese food. A good supply of the right ingredients on your shelves is the best way to induce you to prepare a Chinese meal when you feel you want a change from everyday fare. The Chinese ingredients that are needed in this cookbook for authentic cooking are listed on pages 14–19. One shopping trip, or one order by mail, should provide you with a supply of ingredients adequate to cook Chinese food for a family of four, at least twice a month for a year. In fact, all the Chinese ingredients you will need will fit into a small shopping bag, and they can be stored indefinitely without worrying they will spoil.

All the recipes included use fresh ingredients that are available in most local stores or supermarkets, as well as the Chinese spices and condiments.

Chinese cooking need not be complicated; as you will see, the supplies are readily available, and the rewards are mouth-watering. Get your supply of Chinese ingredients NOW, before you read any further—after you have these basics, go to the supermarket for the other supplies and then rush home and prepare a Chinese feast!

Here's wishing you happy cooking, and as they say in China,

HO YUM HO SIC (good drink, good eat).

May Wong Trent
New York, Hong Kong
1973

Contents

Chinese Cooking Terms

Almost all Chinese dishes are named according to the *way* in which they are cooked; by the main *ingredients* in the dish; and by the specially seasoned *sauce* that is used in the dish. If you have read any Chinese menus or recipes you'll notice that the name of each dish includes these three parts: for example—

> Steamed / sea bass with Chinese mushrooms and scallions / in light soy sauce.

> Stir-fried / flank steak with green peppers / in black bean sauce.

> Braised / beancurd with peas / in oyster sauce

If you understand the cooking terms, then you can easily identify any Chinese dish—cooking method, ingredients, and sauce or seasonings—almost instantly. You'll be able to know just what to expect when you cook, and just what to expect when you order in a restaurant.

The following eight cooking terms will introduce you to Chinese cooking. It is important to learn *all* these terms and to be able to recognize them at sight:

炒 **Stir-fry**   This is the most common method of Chinese cooking. The foods that are to be cooked are usually cut into bite-size pieces and set aside while the oil (peanut oil or vegetable oil) is heated to a sizzle. The bite-size food is added to the hot oil. An even, high heat must be maintained to provide a noisy, constant sizzle throughout the entire stir-frying process. At the same time that the food is frying, the cook must constantly be in action—lifting and turning the ingredients with a spatula. This constant movement, and the sizzling, make a Chinese kitchen a very noisy place. A stir-fried dish should be served immediately after cooking to capture the taste of the freshly cooked food. Ideally, it must not be allowed to sit for even a few minutes.

The flavor and aroma of freshly stir-fried Chinese food is called *wok hay* or *wok flavor*, meaning it is the taste and smell of food that is freshly cooked to perfection, very hot, and cooked with the ideal balance of oil, cooking heat, and timing. Chinese cooks are judged by their *wok flavor* or *wok hay* just as some French cooks are judged by the lightness of their soufflés.

炸 **Deep-fry**   The food is usually dipped in flour or wrapped in dough, and then it is submerged in oil and fried until crisp.

煎 **Shallow-fry**   One side of the food is fried in a thin film of oil until it is brown, then the food is turned onto the other side and fried; shallow-fried food has a crisp outside and a moist inside.

炆 **Braise**   The food is shallow-fried briefly, then water or sauce is added, and the food is stewed in a covered pot until it is tender.

 Red-cook   This is similar to braising, but the liquid added is usually dark soy which gives a reddish brown color to the stewed food.

蒸 **Steam**   The prepared food is seasoned, placed in a heatproof platter, and steamed over a large pot of boiling water. Chinese often economize on fuel by steaming dishes over rice that is being cooked; this way everything is ready at the same time—when the rice is done.

The steaming pot can be a wok with a cover or a large pot with a lid. It must be deep enough to hold the heatproof platter and have good clearance on all sides to allow the steam to circulate around the food.

To steam, place the food in a one to two inch deep heatproof platter or metal pie plate. Put a stand in the pot that is used for steaming. (For this you can use an inverted heatproof bowl. The food platter rests on the stand and must be several inches above the water so that the steam, not boiling water, is cooking the food. See the illustration.) Use about 2 inches of water on the bottom of the pot, and bring the water to a slow boil.

When the water is boiling, place the food platter on the stand, cover the pot and steam the food according to the time specified in the recipe. Keep the water at a steady boil to generate continuous steam.

 Boil   Cook in boiling water. The water should be at a full rolling boil. This method is used for rice, noodles, and dumplings.

 Barbecue   Roast as you would for pork ribs, suckling pigs, chicken, and ducks; in China these foods are usually barbecued by cooking over a braisier, the same results can be achieved in a modern home by roasting in the oven.

In China, it is common practice to buy this barbecued meat all ready for the table from a "cooked meat" store and serve it as it comes from the store. Ready-cooked roast pork is often called for as an ingredient in Chinese dishes.

The eight cooking terms—stir-fry, deep-fry, shallow-fry, braise, red-cook, steam, boil, and barbecue—are arranged according to the time it takes to cook, and how long the dishes are allowed to sit before serving. Stir-fry and deep-fry processes are on the top of the list because they take very little time to cook, and the food must be served as soon as it is cooked. Braising and steaming are further down the list because, using the braising or steaming methods, cooking takes a bit longer and the cooked food can be allowed to sit for some time before serving without losing any of its flavor.

A well-planned Chinese menu should include dishes with three or more different methods of cooking—unless you are prepared to stay in the kitchen and stir-fry away in a frenzy while your family or guests are eating! Clever planning will reduce your last minute cooking chores to only one or two dishes that can be handled easily. This means that in a four-course dinner you should try to include a braised dish (a barbecued duck or chicken from the roast meat shop), a steamed dish (steamed beef or steamed fish), a soup (such as creamed corn egg-drop soup), along with one or two of the fried dishes. (Remember, the steamed dishes will take longer to cook than the fried ones, but the fried dishes will keep you in the kitchen until the very last moment before eating.)

Serve all the food with plain white rice and follow the main dishes with tea, and perhaps some fresh fruit, to complete the meal. The perfect dessert is a cup of Chinese tea.

Cutting

CHOPPING, DICING, SLICING, AND SLANT-CUTTING

Most of the preparation of Chinese food takes place before the actual cooking: to be a Chinese cook you must be fairly good in the cutting of meat, fish, and vegetables. An explanation follows of the four basic cutting techniques—chopping, dicing, slicing, and slant-cutting. The purpose here is to show you what to expect as a result of cutting, not to describe the art of using the meat cleaver. The art of cutting, whether you use a cleaver or a heavy knife, comes only with practice.

You can substitute a heavy knife for the traditional Chinese cleaver and get very good results. Many cooks, and I'm one of them, have a dread fear of the cleaver. But whether you use cleaver or knife, be patient and *practice*. Knowing how to cut quickly and well is basic to Chinese cooking.

Ready, set, *en guard!*

Chopping Use a cleaver or a very heavy knife for this; best results are obtained by holding the knife perpendicular to the cutting board or food. Use an up-and-down motion. Follow the recipe and chop coarsely or finely, according to what is needed.

Dicing   Cut the ingredients into big or small pieces, according to the directions in the recipe.

Slicing   This produces the greatest variety of shapes. Each shape depends on the angle of the slice, and the thickness of the slice, as well as the shape of the meat or vegetable being cut.

   A tip on slicing meat into very thin pieces: Half-freeze the pork, beef, or chicken before slicing. The half-frozen meat will be firm against the knife, but still be cuttable, and will make nice neat slices.

Slant-cut   This is the cut most often used for slicing vegetables. Each knife cut is at an angle, and this will produce a diagonal pointed piece of vegetable instead of a blunt-ended piece. For example, take a piece of *bok choy* (Chinese cabbage) and, instead of cutting it bluntly straight across like this,

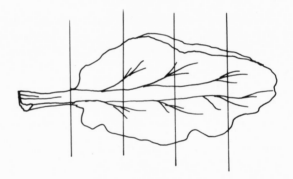

slant-cut the *bok choy* to produce pointed angular pieces. The larger cut surfaces have more exposed area and will absorb seasonings better, and take less time to cook than pieces cut straight across.

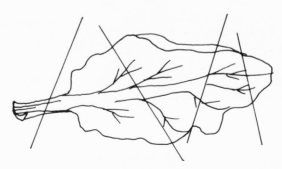

The shapes and sizes of the ingredients that are to be cooked are important factors in any Chinese recipe. Instructions on cutting should be followed exactly. A basic rule to determine the shape and size of ingredients in a dish with two or more ingredients is that they must all be cut to a uniform size and shape. This will ensure an attractive appearance and that all the pieces will cook in about the same time.

For cutting, use the tool that seems the most comfortable to you—a small knife, a cleaver, or a large knife. Then, faithfully copy the shapes recommended for each dish. All the cutting can be finished three or four hours before cooking time.

When everything is cut, use one platter to assemble all the pre-cut ingredients that will be in the same dish. Arrange them so that each ingredient is in a separate heap. Cover the pre-cut, ready-to-cook ingredients with wax paper, foil, or plastic and refrigerate until cooking time.

Because everything can be pre-cut, assembled, and kept in the refrigerator, there is no need for last minute cutting and the food can be cooked quickly and with little fuss.

Equipment, Measures, Temperature

EQUIPMENT

You can probably cook almost any Chinese dish without adding to the pots and pans that are in your kitchen now. However, a *Chinese wok* (with a *wok* cover and special metal collar or ring to adapt it for gas or electric stoves), and a Chinese *spatula* with a raised rim are very handy and make cooking easier for the following reasons:

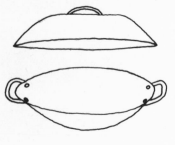

A wok is deep enough to double as a steamer.
In a dish with 2 or more ingredients, food that is completely cooked can be pushed to the upper side of the wok, away from the direct heat to avoid over-cooking.
A wok provides a large cooking surface, ideal for stir-frying bulky cut vegetables.

A spatula with a raised rim is useful for sauces as well as solid food; the food can easily be dished, moved and served.

If you have a large skillet, however, and you are happy with it, use the skillet, it is perfectly suitable. Some cooks prefer a heavy skillet or sturdy frying pan because, they argue, the heat is more evenly distributed than in a wok. Also, as even an empty wok is very heavy, lifting it when it is full can be a strenuous chore, and it does not have an insulated handle for easy gripping.

To season a new wok: wipe it with a damp cloth, and then heat the wok over a high flame. Put about one tablespoon of oil into the wok and swirl the oil around. Heat the oil for about one minute and wipe it all over the wok with a paper towel. Never wash a wok with detergent, steel wool or a wire pad—this will encourage rust. After each use, just rinse in hot water and, if scrubbing is necessary, use a stiff nylon brush while the wok is still hot.

It's important to have a good chopper or *heavy knife* (see page 5) for effective chopping. The *Chinese cleaver* has an extra broad blade that is excellent for transferring food from the cutting board or work area to the wok or

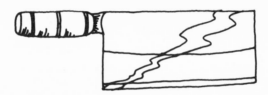

skillet. It can also be used for crushing garlic and ginger by banging the broad blade of the cleaver smartly on the garlic clove or ginger root to flatten and smash it.

MEASURES

In Chinese cooking, measures do not have to be absolutely exact. Chinese dishes are not based on fixed measurements, like a cake or soufflé. Having the ingredients cut in the correct shapes is the main consideration. After that, it is up to you how salty, hot, or spicy you want the food to be. So, if the recipe calls for one teaspoon of hot sauce, you can double that amount if your family and guests like very hot, spicy food. This advice applies to all seasoning. But the first few times you make a dish, do exercise restraint when altering or substituting the amount of seasonings. Measure roughly, yes, but not too, too rough!

TEMPERATURES FOR COOKING

Chinese cooking is not concerned wtih exact temperatures as measured by the degrees on a thermometer: Read the section on cooking terms again (pages 2–3), and use this simple guide:

Stir-fry The mixture should be sizzling and simmering all the time.

Deep-fry As the term suggests, hot oil is used and the technique is similar to the way you would fry french fried potatoes.

Shallow-fry Deep sizzle, just as in pan-frying sausages.

Braise and Red-cook Cook at a simmer, with little bubbles around the edges of the pan.

Steam Water is at a slow rolling boil to maintain continuous steam.

Boil Water should be bubbling rapidly.

The Indispensable Chopsticks

快
子

In most Chinese homes, each family member has his own pair of chopsticks. When I was about four and just learning to feed myself, I had a very short pair of plastic chopsticks about six inches long, with pointed tips for spearing food. Then, when I was about ten, I was given standard length chopsticks, about ten inches long, made of ivory and with my name carved on them in Chinese characters. By the time I was fifteen, these ivory chopsticks were pretty well chewed up and were yellowing with age. I then inherited a slender silver pair from my older sister. These didn't last very long; the tips stained easily and there were teethmarks all over the soft silver. My mother then gave me a set of her chopsticks which were made of ivory and had her name on them, with a little family crest inlaid in red lacquer at the top.

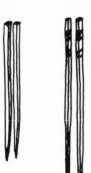

At dinner time in a Chinese family, the table is set with chopsticks that are made from many different materials—bamboo, wood, ivory, silver, plastic or bone. They will be in all colors and sizes—from six inches to ten inches in length, and in many shapes—round, square, combination, rounded tips, or pointed tips. In our family, the only time when all the chopsticks on the table are of a uniform design and length is when guests are invited. I think food tastes best with my own personal pair of chopsticks.

Chopsticks have a long tradition, and many interesting customs and beliefs are associated with them. *Chopsticks* in Chinese means "quick little boys." They are considered a very suitable gift for newlyweds because chopsticks carry with them the wish for a speedy addition to the family.

Chinese folklore also says you can predict how far away a girl's husband will come from by the way she holds the chopsticks; the further away from the eating end that the chopsticks are held, the more distant will be the native land of her husband and her future home.

Chopsticks and porcelain spoons are the two utensils that the Chinese use to feed themselves. The spoons are for soup, for sauces, and to scoop finely chopped-up food from dishes to rice bowls. The chopsticks do the rest of the work—from shoveling rice into our mouths (rice is rarely picked up, it is usually pushed into the mouth with the chopsticks), to picking up and discarding bones, to cutting up food, or dividing up food.

In cooking, we use chopsticks of wood or bamboo because they are heat resistant. You will find chopsticks ideal for stirring, mixing, tasting, and even for beating eggs. I use them for cooking more than I use any other utensils—even when I cook French or Italian food. Bits of food don't adhere easily to chopsticks, so they don't drip. Chopsticks can be rested on the rims of cups or plates so that the soiled part of the sticks never touches anything.

In general, most Americans agree chopsticks are neat and a dandy piece of equipment—once you learn to use them!

For those of you who haven't yet mastered the art of holding chopsticks, here is a step-by-step teach-yourself guide:

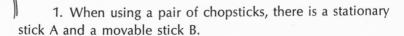

1. When using a pair of chopsticks, there is a stationary stick A and a movable stick B.

2. The crook of the thumb and finger 4 are for resting the stationary chopstick A.

3. The tips of thumb, finger 2 and finger 3 are used for grasping movable stick B and moving it up and down.

When chopsticks are in use, the palm of your hand should be facing you while the back of your hand is away from you.

Ingredients for Chinese Cooking and Mail Order Sources

BOTTLED AND CANNED SAUCES

The following is a list of traditional Chinese condiments, sauces, and spices. These can be ordered from the suppliers on page 19, or in some cities, many of these ingredients are available in local stores and supermarkets.

Dark Soy Dark soy is made from fermented soybeans, wheat, salt, and yeast. Dark soy is a dark-brown liquid that usually comes in a tall, slender bottle. Stored in its bottle, it will keep forever.

Light Soy Like the dark soy, is made from beans, wheat, salt and yeast. It is light-brown in color and less intense in flavor than the dark soy.

Hoisin Sauce A brownish-red paste made from soybeans, sugar, garlic, flour, and spices. It tastes a bit like ketchup, and it is used as a dip and in cooking. It will store indefinitely in a tightly sealed jar.

Oyster Sauce A thick brown sauce made from oysters, sugar, and soy sauce. It will keep indefinitely in a cool place.

Fish Sauce Fish sauce is a light-brown thin liquid made from extracts of fish, water and salt. It will keep indefinitely.

Hot Red Chili Oil This red spicy oil is extremely hot. It is made from chili and oil. It keeps indefinitely in your refrigerator.

Sesame Oil A brownish oil with a strong aroma made from sesame seeds. It is quite viscous and it will keep indefinitely.

Hot Brown Bean Sauce *(Dow Barn Jeung)* is a thick brown bean paste with chili and garlic. It is very hot and often used in Szechuan cooking. It is packaged in a bottle or can, and keeps on the shelf indefinitely.

Chinese Rice Wine is a strong white liquor that is quite different from the mild yellow variety of Chinese wine. Store it in a cool place.

Salted Black Beans   Dry black beans that are sold and stored in plastic bags. They can be left in the plastic bags for about a year, or once the bags are opened, you can keep them in a tightly sealed jar for years.

Chinese Mushrooms   These are mushrooms that have been dried and preserved. They are usually sold in plastic bags or containers. They can be stored indefinitely. To prepare, soak them until they are soft and then remove the stumps before use. Use only the umbrella or cap section of the mushroom.

5 Spice Powder   This is a combination of powdered spices that are sold in small paper packets. The mixture includes anise, fennel, Szechuan pepper, cloves, and cinnamon. Stored in an air-tight jar, it will keep indefinitely.

Star Anise   The small blossoms of the anise plant that look like brown stars are sold in plastic bags. Stored in the bags, or a tightly sealed jar, they will last indefinitely.

Dry Shrimps   The small shrimp that have been dried from sea water. They are usually sold in plastic bags. They will keep indefinitely.

Beanthread or Cellophane Noodles The white, thread-like noodles made from ground mung beans. They are sold in bundles and packed in plastic bags. They keep forever. To use, cover with water and soak the beanthread noodles until they are soft.

Egg Noodles The long, thin noodles made of flour and eggs. They are wound in yellow cake forms, dried and sold in bags of six to eight cakes. They keep well for at least a year.

Rice Stick Noodles These are very much like beanthread noodles, but are made from ground rice. They keep well for about a year.

CANNED VEGETABLES

Bamboo Shoots Young white plants about an inch long. They are sold in cans either whole or sliced. After you've opened the can, use the contents within a week. Store the contents of an opened can, well covered, in your refrigerator.

Pickled Turnip Heads (Kohlrabi) These root vegetables are hot, spicy and salty. They are sold with six to eight turnip heads packed in each can. You can store the turnips forever, if you keep them in tightly sealed jars in the refrigerator.

Vegetable Steaks or Mock Abalone This is small preserved beancurd made from wheat gluten. It is sold in cans. Use the entire contents of the can after opening; it does not store well once opened.

FRESH PERISHABLES

Fresh Ginger Root Ginger is sold by the piece. It keeps for months in jars and will keep even longer if peeled and immersed in sherry.

Beancurd A fresh, custard-like soybean product, which is sold in squares. It is stored in barrels in the shop and sold by the piece. It must be used within two or three days of purchase.

Roast Pork Roast pork is sold by weight in Chinese grocery stores or meat stores. It can be kept in the refrigerator for about one week. You can make your own roast pork by following the recipe given on page 82.

Beansprouts The tiny white sprouts of the mung bean. They are sold fresh from barrels and usually measured by weight. Use them up within three to four days. Canned beansprouts are not as crisp or sweet as the fresh. It's fun to grow your own.

Pickled Mustard Green The stem is stained yellowish green during pickling. It is stored in brine in barrels and sold by the piece. Store in jars for up to a month.

Bok Choy *Bok choy* has long white stalks and large green leaves; it is sold fresh by weight, or by the bundle. You can keep it fresh for about a week by storing it in a plastic bag in the vegetable section of your refrigerator.

Chinese Celery Cabbage This cabbage has wide white stalks with crinkled yellow-white leaves. Store just as you would *bok choy.*

Snow Peas Snow peas are flat green beans about three inches long. They are sweet and crisp.

Winter Melon A winter melon is a melon with a dark-green skin, white meat and large yellow seeds. It is sold fresh by the whole melon or by the slice. Use it within two or three days.

MAIL ORDER SOURCES FOR DRY INGREDIENTS

East Coast

New York City
S. Y. Wong, Inc.
28 East Broadway
New York, N.Y. 10022

Yuet Hing Market Corp.
23 Pell Street
New York, N.Y. 10013

Boston
Wing Wing Imported Groceries
79 Harrison Avenue
Boston, Massachusetts 02111

Washington, D.C.
Tack Cheong Company
617 H Street N.W.
Washington, D.C.

Midwest

Star Market
3349 North Clark Street
Chicago, Illinois 60657

Texas
Oriental Import/Export Company
2009 Polk Street
Houston, Texas 77002

California
Wing Chong Lung
922 South Pedro Street
Los Angeles, California 90015

Shing Chong & Company
800 Grant Avenue
San Francisco, California 94108

As I said before, if you order all of the dry ingredients you need for a year, the entire bulk will be less than one shopping bag. The cost of the items vary from ten cents to a dollar.

The fresh ingredients listed can be bought from a Chinese grocery store. The only ingredient you'll need at all times is fresh ginger. Read more about ginger on page 23. The other fresh ingredients are required in fewer than ten percent of the recipes. So, you can actually make almost all of the recipes given here without shopping in Chinatown, once you have ordered and assembled your dry ingredients. A supply of ingredients should encourage you to cook Chinese food often; you won't have the excuse of not having the time to shop!

THE CHINESE GROCERY STORE

Probably at this point the question in your mind is: where shall I go to buy my ingredients if I don't want to use a mail order house, and I really want to go to a Chinese grocery store? Wonderful! You already have the spirit to get right into things. Take a trip to Chinatown, to the nearest cluster of Chinese stores, or even a Japanese store if that's the only oriental shop near you.

You cannot fail to recognize a Chinese grocery store. The exotic and unfamiliar ingredients literally spill out into the sidewalk and press against display windows. Under one roof you will find the dry goods, sauces, spices, canned goods, fresh vegetables, fish, meat, roast meat—everything. You may see a foki* scaling a live fish, another helper may be chopping up a whole roast duck, or halving a suckling pig. The vegetables can be touched and inspected before you buy.

The attraction in shopping in Chinatown is that you need to visit only one shop to assemble all your Chinese cooking ingredients. Some ingredients like beancurd, beansprout or pickled mustard greens may not be in sight; they are usually kept hidden in tall wooden barrels in a dark corner. So if you don't see what you want, ask the shopkeeper.

To point you in the general direction where the grocery stores are clustered in New York's Chinatown, walk along Mott, Bayard or Mulberry Streets. Pay a special visit to the big stores:

> Wing Woh Lung at 50 Mott Street, for everything from fish to snow peas.
> Han May Meat Co. at 69 Mulberry Street for their famous barbecued meat, especially roast pork.
> King Chong Co. at 82 Bayard Street for fresh seafood. Their live crabs are very meaty and fresh.

*A foki 伙 記 means "one who keeps the account"; in a shop, it is the saleshelp, in a restaurant it is the waiter. Never refer to the chief, boss, or owner as the foki, it would be impolite to do this.

Chinese ingredients can include over 100 items, when rare and bizarre dishes are cooked. I've listed 20 ingredients here plus some fresh vegetables. (Please notice that MSG is not recommended at all.)

A good solid cook with a small repertoire of perfectly prepared recipes is far superior to the cook who is trapped in a half-knowledge of many complex dishes. A Chinese gourmand, when hiring his personal chef, usually asks for only three simple test dishes to determine the cook's skill—stir-fried beef, steamed ground pork, and an egg-drop soup. These simple dishes prove whether or not the cook can use the basic techniques of Chinese cooking to prepare simple but perfect dishes distinguished by their flavor, not by their rare ingredients or complex preparations.

On Oil, Soy, Ginger and Scallions, and Chinese Dried Mushrooms

FOUR RULES

A new Chinese cook should remember these four rules—

1. Choose your oil wisely
2. Differentiate between dark and light soy
3. Always use fresh ginger and fresh scallions
4. Chinese dry mushrooms must be soaked in water to soften before using.

OIL

In Chinese cooking, always use either peanut or vegetable oil because they are odorless in cooking. Do not use olive oil, and avoid lard or prepared shortening such as Crisco. Shortenings tend to make the cooked dishes smell slightly oily and rancid.

Whenever oil is used in the actual cooking, always heat the oil until it sizzles *before* adding any ingredients. When the oil is sizzling hot, there is no greasy taste from the raw oil. Chinese cooks swear by "cooking" the oil first.

SOY SAUCES

Be aware of the difference between light and dark soy. Using Japanese soy sauce will give you a Sino-Nippon dish. Please try to avoid it. Use Chinese soy which comes in two strengths: the dark soy and the light soy. Their taste is completely different. Confucius did not say that light soy is dark soy plus water! In fact, dark soy used on certain stir-fried dishes calling for light soy will impart an unpleasant sour and bitter taste.

GINGER AND SCALLIONS

Always use fresh ginger and fresh scallions; never use prepared ginger powder, it's just not Chinese. The fresh ginger has two functions: to season the food, and to rid the oil and food of any raw taste.

There's no substitute for fresh ginger in actual seasoning. You'll have to use the real thing or forget about making a dish that calls for ginger.

When you use the recipes, you'll notice that very often two slices of fresh ginger are added to the oil that is heated before the actual cooking. The ginger is used here to dispel the oily taste and to bring out the fresh taste of the main ingredients. It has little value for seasoning as such.

If you don't have fresh ginger in the house, you can still make that particular dish. Sometimes when I run out of ginger (it's not supposed to happen to any self-respecting Chinese cook, but it does), I substitute the white sections of fresh scallions, or one-half of a clove of garlic, and heat it in the oil.

Fresh ginger can be kept indefinitely in a tightly covered jar filled with water or sherry. If you keep the ginger in water, the water must be changed about once a week. If it is peeled and kept in sherry, it is not necessary to renew the sherry.

If you are not storing the ginger in sherry, it's not necessary to peel it unless sand and mud cover the skin. When a recipe calls for thin slices of ginger, just slice the ginger thinly, crosswise, holding the knife at a right angle to the ginger to make slices that are about one-eighth-inch thick and roughly one inch in diameter.

Scallions required in Chinese cooking should always be fresh. Wash and clean the scallions in running water, discard any wilted leaves and cut away the roots before using. Scallions have three uses:

> — cut in short strips, they're used at the start of cooking in hot sizzling oil to dispel any oily taste (the same function as ginger).
> — chopped fine, or in thin strips, they are used as seasoning.
> — cut in one-eighth-inch rings, they are used as garnishes for cooked dishes.

CHINESE DRIED MUSHROOMS

These dry black caps are sold in plastic bags (see page 16) and keep forever. They must be soaked in water for about one-half hour to soften them before use. Chinese mushrooms are one of the most versatile and useful accompaniments for almost anything from a pork dish to a soup dish. They must be used sparingly, because they're very expensive and a little goes a long way—they have a strong flavor, however, so only a few mushrooms are usually required. A good tip in using up a bag of dry mushrooms is to take the oddly shaped and small mushrooms when you need mushrooms cut into quarters or strips, and to save the perfect round caps for dishes that call for whole mushrooms.

CHINESE SAUCES

Let's solve the mystery of Chinese sauces. The Chinese sauce is quite unlike its complicated French cousin. Basically, the Chinese sauce is a liquid with a thickening made of cornstarch dissolved in a mixture of water and soy and is used to glaze and bind the food. Dark soy is used chiefly for dark meat, such as beef, and light soy is used for white meat, such as chicken, vegetables or fish. Usually, just before the dish has finished cooking, the sauce is added to the food and everything is simmered until thickened—usually only a few seconds. There's no chance of ruining or curdling a Chinese sauce. The cornstarch will always thicken when simmered.

Adding ingredients to this cornstarch and soy mixture is the way to make fancy sauces such as lobster sauce, oyster sauce, sweet-and-sour sauce, hot Szechuan sauce, and so forth. Most of these extra ingredients come ready-made from a bottle! Here is a description of a few sauces:

> **Basic Sauce**   Cornstarch, water, and soy.
>
> **Oyster Sauce**   The sauce comes ready-made from a bottle. It is thick and very well seasoned, and can therefore be used alone as a complete sauce. A more common practice is to mix it with the basic sauce of cornstarch, water, and soy to make a larger quantity that has a more modest flavor than the straight-from-the-bottle strong oyster flavor of the sauce when used alone.
>
> **Sweet and Sour Sauce**   This is made by combining the basic sauce with vinegar and sugar. Sometimes diced carrots, green peppers, or pineapples are added for a special taste or effect.

Hot Brown Bean and Chili Sauce   This is a thick paste made of mashed brown beans and chili with some additional red chili oil. It is packed in jars. There are many different brands of hot chili sauce or brown bean sauce on the market. Any brand will do as they all taste very much the same. Most hot spicy Szechuan dishes are made by adding this to the basic sauce.

Lobster Sauce   Note that there is no lobster in this sauce. It gets its name because lobster is sometimes cooked in a similar sauce. This sauce is a mixture of the basic sauce, fermented black beans, beaten egg whites, garlic, scallions and stock. Ground pork can be added to this sauce for additional texture and flavor.

Master Sauce   The main sauce in each recipe in this book is referred to as the Master Sauce. This Master Sauce is mixed in advance in a bowl or cup by combining various ingredients like soy, cornstarch, sugar, salt, pepper, sesame oil, plus any other sauces. No two Master Sauces are alike as you'll notice when you read the recipes. The only similarity is that Master Sauce means you'll have a sauce premixed in a cup ready to add to the other ingredients when you start to cook. The Chinese often call this the "bowl sauce."

How to Make Friends in a Chinese Restaurant

The Chinese in the restaurant business are very sensitive to the wishes of their patrons. They take great pride in their work, and in their knowledge of food and cooking. Chinese cooks and waiters have a tradition that goes back thousands of years. No matter how good one is at restaurant etiquette, there's usually some small nuance of etiquette of which you are unaware, and even a single blunder can reduce you, in the eyes of the restaurant staff, to an ignorant person—to be tolerated and humored, but not respected. Ordering a bit from there and a bit from here—without a plan—can be just that Chinese restaurant *faux pas*.

In a very large restaurant, or a fancy restaurant, you might give your order to the "host" or manager. In most Chinese restaurants, however, you would deal with a *foki,* as a waiter in a restaurant is called. The *foki* is responsible for serving you, and he is very sensitive to the reactions of his clients. The *foki* will disappear from the table, not to return, if anything is said about the food, service, or atmosphere that reflects negatively on the restaurant, or any disparaging comments are made that can be interpreted as a direct insult, so be careful; lost face is face lost forever!

The dignified way to establish rapport in a Chinese restaurant is to behave as you would if you were talking to a helpful and knowledgeable maître d'hôtel. You shouldn't put yourself entirely in his hands, looking helpless and pathetic as some experts would advise you (if you did this, the *foki* might consider you ignorant). As for the *foki*'s recommendation; accept dishes which appeal to you but, at the same time, do not hesitate to ask for your favorite dishes.

After you have studied the menu, put it aside; look around for posted paper strips with Chinese brushwork characters. These are the specialties of the season and of that day. If you get a chance, look at what is being eaten by other patrons. For eight people, order five to six dishes. Aim for a balanced menu with a good variety of meat, seafood, vegetables, and other ingredients. These dishes are brought to the tables at the same time and shared by all of the guests in the same party.

Get organized before the *foki* appears at your table. Only one person should do the ordering for the group. He should ask each member of the party what he would like. You should start ordering as soon as possible after the *foki* appears at the table. All Chinese restaurants work with "chop-chop" haste.

Here is how you order: Start by naming your preference, say a crunchy vegetable dish. Ask what kind of fresh vegetables are in season. He'll tell you; if it seems appealing, take his suggestions.

Then, ask him about the dishes advertised on the wall. Tell the *foki* what the choices of the group may be—shrimp, beancurd, etc.—and ask if they're available from the wall menu. In this way you'll get one or two dishes that are prepared as specialties of the house.

If you have trouble remembering the name of a particular dish you might have had elsewhere, or read about, describe the ingredients in the dish, the way the sauce looked, and the taste of the dish. The *foki* will usually be able to help you by naming the dish, or suggesting an alternative selection that you might also like.

There is usually a special house soup of the day; this is almost always good. So, if you're ordering soup, ask first for the house soup to see if you like it. If you settle for the house soup, it will probably be brought immediately.

Perhaps you notice another patron eating an interesting dish. Instead of pointing and say, "What's that?" try to recognize the ingredients in the dish, and ask the *foki* if it is made with chicken (for example), and how it has been prepared. He'll be glad to tell you all about the dish, and recommend it if it goes with the other entrées that are ordered.

The next step is to count the dishes you've ordered. If you've lost track, the *foki* will tell you, and let you know if there is enough for everyone. End the friendly ordering by saying: *Ngmm goy nay* which means "thank you," and then ask for hot tea, plain rice with the food, or any special service such as warming the rice wine.

This is an accepted way of ordering in a Chinese restaurant—plenty of discussion between the *foki* and the patron. The patron gets what he wants, and the *foki* has provided information about the vegetables in season, the soup of the day, the specialties of the house, the dishes that the other patrons were eating. The exchange has been happy and amiable.

Many Chinese restaurants do not have a liquor license, but they'll gladly accept any wine or liquors you've brought with you, and provide glasses and service. Chinese rice wine, served warm, will show the *foki* that you understand Chinese tradition. And the *foki* will approve. The rice wine can be bought from nearby liquor stores.

How to Use the Recipes

Before you start Chinese cooking, please remember that you're using basically the same cooking techniques that enable you to prepare any other kind of food. The difference is that now you're going to cook three or four dishes at a sitting, instead of the usual single main course. This multi-course dinner, served all at once, requires a logical organization of recipes for a reasonable division of time and labor in the kitchen. This will enable you to produce the dishes, ready to serve and piping hot, without the food being ruined by bad timing in cooking, by waiting and getting cold, and without your becoming agitated, anxious and harried.

To help you cook the dishes properly, we have arranged the recipes so that the preparation of the ingredients can be easily read and completely finished without your having to turn the page.

FORMAT AND PLAN OF THE RECIPES

Title This tells the method of cooking, the main ingredients, and the sauce.

Ingredients   They are listed in the sequence that corresponds to the step-by-step preparation and cooking instructions which follow.

Preparation   This part should be done three to four hours before the actual cooking. It involves cutting, assembling the ingredients, and then covering and storing the semi-prepared food in the refrigerator until cooking time.

Illustrations   This section shows how each ingredient should be cut and what the raw assembled ingredients are like. When necessary, unusual cooking or serving methods are shown in the illustrations.

Cooking   An approximate cooking time is given for each dish, indicated by the clock on the top left corner of the recipe.

Cooking steps   These are numbered to make the steps easy to follow.

Serving suggestions   This section tells you how to serve the food generally, and how to serve some special Chinese dish in the traditional way.

Yield   This refers to the number of servings per dish. Each recipe can feed six people in a dinner if it is accompanied by three other dishes. When you are experimenting with one dish it will serve two adequately.

General notes   These include how long the dish can sit, or if it can be reheated; ingredient substitutes, if there are any; folklore or anecdotes about the dish.

A FEW FINAL SUGGESTIONS AND REMINDERS

In stir-frying, keep the flame high enough, and the oil sufficiently hot to seal in the juices. Eat the dish while it is hot enough to capture the "wok flavor" or *wok hay* (鑊氣).

If a dish must be marinated briefly before cooking, the Chinese will throw the cornstarch, soy, etc., right on the meat, then use their fingers or chopsticks to mix *well*. Cornstarch does not form lumps like flour.

When using cornstarch to thicken the sauce, add the cornstarch only when the sauce is sizzling, and serve the dish after the cornstarch has simmered and thickened. Work quickly always, be ready by knowing the next step in the cooking—before you get to it. Make *wok hay* while the food sizzles!

Here's wishing you happy cooking and *Ho yum, ho sic*—Good drinking, good eating!

Soups

INTRODUCTION

Chinese soups can be divided roughly into three kinds. First are the "healthy" soups—these are brewed for hours, the chief ingredients being meat, fowl or vegetables, or a combination. Salt is the only seasoning. This kind of slowly brewed, clear, rich broth forms part of the Chinese family's diet and is served a few times a month. It is believed that taking it regularly will ensure general well-being (similar to taking vitamins), prevent colds, and that "run-down" feeling, and fatigue.

Second is the clear appetizing soup which takes less than one-half hour to prepare. The base, which can be canned chicken broth or water, is brought to a boil, then fresh vegetables, pieces of meat, etc. are added to be cooked briefly. When made with green vegetables, the soup is very refreshing and has a "cooling" effect, whereas when pickled vegetables are used, it is spicy and piquant.

Third are the thick spicy soups that also take less than half an hour to prepare. Again the base can be canned chicken broth, or water. Slivers of meat, vegetables, beancurd, mushrooms and almost any other ingredients are cooked quickly in the stock, thus enriching it with many flavors. Then cornstarch, or sometimes beaten eggs, are added as a thickener. Sometimes hot oil, vinegar, and sesame oil are added to give the thickened soup that extra lift. This soup is not in the "healthy" category because it has a short cooking period; and is not frequently served at home to the family. However, its spiciness is a great appetizer for the beginning of a meal and is ordered often when the family is eating out. Herein lies the Chinese belief that restaurants will seldom take the time and trouble to brew a "healthy" soup. As nothing is worse than half-brewed or "short-cut" soup, we would rather order the spicy soups and trust the "healthy" soups to home cooking.

Guests in a Chinese home served with a "healthy" soup (*Bo Tong* [保湯], *bo* means healthy and *tong* means soup) may find it less tasty than the spicy appetizing kinds (full of MSG!) which they get in a restaurant. Do remember, then, that the hostess has taken the trouble to serve you with a superior soup which is doing great things to your body.

Chinese soups can be served before, during, or at the end of the meal. It is sipped at random, so feel free to take a few spoonfuls, put the soup aside, and come back to it later. When you drink soup, do it native-style; bring the bowl to the lips and sip, instead of spooning it.

10 MINUTES
COOKING TIME

CREAMED CORN

EGG-DROP SOUP

INGREDIENTS:

one 12-oz. can clear chicken broth
one 16-oz. can creamed corn
2 cups water

—

2 eggs

—

3 pieces scallions, cut into ⅛" rings
salt and pepper to taste

TO PREPARE:

1. Beat eggs well, set aside.
2. Slice scallions into ⅛" rings.

TO COOK: (*cooking time about 10 minutes*)

1. Bring to boil chicken broth, creamed corn, and water.
2. Keep the soup boiling, add the beaten eggs and stir vigorously with chopsticks or whisk to cook eggs. Do not overcook. Cooking time should be less than 1 minute.
3. Add the chopped scallions. Season the soup with salt and pepper. Serve.
4. To serve: Serve hot in soup bowls. This dish should be served at once so that eggs are not overcooked.
5. Yield: Serves 6.

10 MINUTES
COOKING TIME

WATERCRESS AND
PORK SLICES SOUP

INGREDIENTS:

2 pork chops, cut into ⅛" slices
1 teaspoon cornstarch
1 tablespoon light soy
1 teaspoon sesame oil

—

5 cups water
1 tablespoon peanut or vegetable oil
1 teaspoon salt
2 thin slices fresh ginger

—

¼ lb. fresh watercress
salt to taste

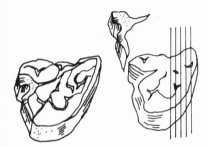

TO PREPARE:

1. Trim and discard bones of pork chops. Lay chops flat and cut crosswise into ⅛" slices. Put in a bowl, add cornstarch, light soy and sesame oil, mix well, marinate ½ hour.

2. Cut 2 thin slices fresh ginger.

3. Wash and drain watercress, cut into 2" pieces.

TO COOK: *(cooking time about 10 minutes)*

1. In a large pot bring to boil water, oil, salt, and ginger.

2. Add marinated pork slices and *boil* uncovered 5 minutes.

3. Keep soup boiling, add watercress, and boil 3 minutes more. Season by salting to taste. Serve.

4. To serve: Serve hot in individual bowls. Each serving contains soup, watercress and pork slices. This soup can sit covered in its pot for about 1 hour. To serve, reheat gently and serve hot. Do not overboil watercress or it will turn yellow and lose its crispness.

5. Yield: Serves 6.

BEEF AND SPINACH

SOUP

**10 MINUTES
COOKING TIME**

INGREDIENTS:

    ½ lb. fresh spinach

—

    6 cups water
    2 thin slices fresh ginger
    1 tablespoon peanut or vegetable oil
    1 teaspoon salt

—

    ½ lb. flank steak
    1 teaspoon cornstarch
    1 tablespoon light soy
    1 tablespoon peanut or vegetable oil
    ½ teaspoon sugar
    dash white pepper

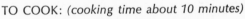

TO PREPARE:

    1. Wash and cut spinach leaves in 2" lengths.

    2. Cut 2 thin slices fresh ginger.

    3. Lay flank steak flat, halve it lengthwise, and cut crosswise into ⅛" slices.

    4. Mix beef slices with cornstarch, light soy, oil, sugar, and pepper. Marinate ½ hour.

TO COOK: *(cooking time about 10 minutes)*

    1. In a heavy pot bring to boil water, ginger, oil, and salt.

    2. Add spinach and boil uncovered 3 minutes.

    3. Keep soup boiling, add marinated beef slices, boil and stir 1 minute. Serve.

    4. To serve: Serve hot at once in individual soup bowls. This soup cannot sit, for beef will be overcooked and tough, and spinach will lose its greenness.

    5. Yield: Serves 6.

    Notes: Other vegetables suitable for this soup are any of the green-leaved ones like *bok choy*, Chinese broccoli and mustard greens.

**20 MINUTES
COOKING TIME**

FRESH LETTUCE

AND BEANCURD SOUP

INGREDIENTS:

· *one 12-oz. can clear chicken broth*
2 cans water

—

4 pieces fresh beancurds, cut into 1" pieces
2 thin slices fresh ginger
1 teaspoon salt

—

1 small head fresh lettuce

TO PREPARE:

1. Cut beancurd into 1" cubes.
2. Cut 2 thin slices fresh ginger.
3. Separate the leaves of lettuce. Wash and drain. Cut the leaves crosswise into halves.

TO COOK: *(cooking time about 20 minutes)*

1. Bring to boil the chicken broth and water.
2. Add beancurds, ginger and salt. Cover pot and simmer 10 minutes.
3. Remove cover, bring soup to a rapid boil, and add all the lettuce. Let boil 1 minute. Add more salt if necessary. Serve.
4. To serve: Serve hot at once in individual soup bowls. The soup can be made more than an hour before serving; but do not add the lettuce. Just before serving, bring to a boil and add lettuce. Adding the lettuce at the last minute preserves its crunchy texture and green color.

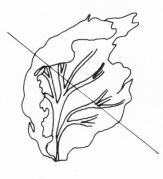

**2 HOURS
COOKING TIME**

CHINESE MUSHROOM SOUP

WITH CHICKEN FEET

INGREDIENTS:

> *2 thin slices fresh ginger*
> *8 cups water*
> —
> *5 pairs chicken feet*
> *10 Chinese mushrooms, soaked in water till soft*
> —
> *salt to taste*

TO PREPARE:

1. Cut 2 thin slices fresh ginger.
2. Wash chicken feet. Chop away the toes.
3. Discard stems of softened mushrooms.

TO COOK: *(cooking time about 2 hours)*

1. Put water in a large heavy pot, add ginger, cover and bring to a boil.

2. Add chicken feet and mushrooms. Lower flame, cover pot, and simmer 2 hours. Make sure there are always about 6 cups of water in pot. Add more water if necessary.

3. To serve: Season with salt to taste, serve hot in bowls with chicken feet and mushrooms in each serving. This soup can be made hours before serving and reheated.

4. Yield: Serves 6-8.

Notes: For the squeamish, wings or other parts of the chicken may be substituted for the chicken feet.

PIGS' FEET SOUP

WITH RAW PEANUTS

2½ HOURS
COOKING TIME

INGREDIENTS:

2 pigs' feet, cut into 2" pieces

—

10 cups water

—

1 whole pickled mustard green

—

1 cup raw skinned peanuts
20 whole black peppercorns

—

salt and black pepper to taste

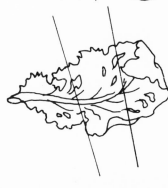

TO PREPARE:

1. Chop pigs' feet into 2" pieces.
2. Wash mustard green, separate stalks, cut into 1" pieces.

TO COOK: (*cooking time about 2½ hours*)

1. In a large pot cover pigs' feet with 10 cups cold water. Bring to boil and boil 10 minutes.

2. Using a ladle, skim off about 2 cups liquid to discard all scum. Return to boil.

3. Add pickled mustard green, peanuts and peppercorns. Cover pot and simmer for 2½ hours or until pigs' feet are tender. Add more water if necessary to make sure there are always 8 cups of liquid in the pot.

4. Season with salt and black pepper. Serve hot.

5. To serve: Serve hot in individual soup bowls. Each serving should contain 1 piece pigs' feet, some pickled mustard green and peanuts. This dish can sit for hours. Reheat to serve.

6. Yield: Serves 6-8.

DICED WINTER MELON SOUP

WITH SMALL SHRIMPS

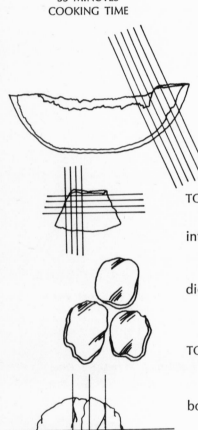

55 MINUTES
COOKING TIME

INGREDIENTS:

one 12-oz. can clear chicken broth
2 cans water

—

1-lb. slice of winter melon, peeled
3 thin slices fresh ginger
6 Chinese mushrooms, soaked in water till soft

—

½ lb. small shrimps, shelled

—

dash white pepper
salt to taste

TO PREPARE:

1. Seed, peel and cut winter melon into ¼″ slices. Dice into ¼″ cubes.
2. Cut 3 thin slices fresh ginger.
3. Discard stems and cut softened mushrooms into ¼″ dices.
4. Shell shrimps and cut into ¼″ pieces.

TO COOK: *(cooking time about 55 minutes)*

1. Bring to boil chicken broth and water in a large pot.
2. Add winter melon, ginger, and mushrooms. Bring to boil, cover pot, and simmer ¾ hour.
3. Add shrimps, cover pot and simmer 5 minutes.
4. Season with white pepper and salt, serve.
5. To serve: Serve hot in individual soup bowls. The soup can sit in the pot for hours before the shrimps are added. Serve at once when everything is ready or the shrimps will be overcooked and turn fishy.
6. Yield: Serves 6.

Notes: Winter melon is available only in Chinese grocery stores. It is sold by the slice and will keep for about two days in the refrigerator. There is no substitute for it.

20 MINUTES
COOKING TIME

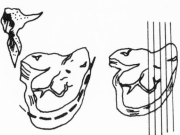

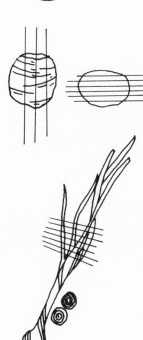

CHINESE PICKLED

KOHLRABI SOUP

INGREDIENTS:

one 12-oz. can clear chicken broth
3 cans water
—

2 thin pork chops, cut into thin strips
2 pickled kohlrabi heads, cut into thin strips
—

2 ozs. cellophane noodles, soaked in water until soft
—

2 pieces scallions, cut into ⅛″ rings
salt and white pepper to taste (see Notes)

TO PREPARE:

1. Cut away and discard the bones of each pork chop. Trim excess fat. Lay the chops on a flat board and split them horizontally in halves. You will then have 4 very thin chops. Cut each into thin strips about ⅛″ wide.

2. Wash kohlrabi heads in water (there are about 6 heads in each can, the rest can keep forever in jars in the refrigerator). Cut each head into ⅛″ slices, then into thin strips.

3. Cover cellophane noodles with water and soak until soft.

4. Cut scallions into ⅛″ rings.

TO COOK: *(cooking time about 20 minutes)*

1. In a large pot bring to boil the chicken broth and water.

2. Add pork and kohlrabi strips and simmer 15 minutes.

3. Add cellophane noodles and simmer 2 minutes.

4. Add scallion rings, stir to mix. Season with salt and pepper. Serve.

5. To serve: Serve hot in individual soup bowls. The soup can sit for hours if the cellophane noodles and scallions are not added. Serve immediately after the cellophane noodles and scallions have been added.

6. Yield: Serves 6.

Notes: The pickled kohlrabi is very salty. Add salt only if needed.

10 MINUTES
COOKING TIME

FISH AND LETTUCE SOUP

WITH CHRYSANTHEMUM PETALS

INGREDIENTS:

one 12-oz. can clear chicken broth
3 cans water
6 thin slices fresh ginger
1 tablespoon peanut or vegetable oil

—

1 small lettuce

—

½ lb. fillet of flounder
20 chrysanthemum flower petals, fresh

—

salt and white pepper to taste

TO PREPARE:

1. Cut thin slices fresh ginger.
2. Separate stalks and wash lettuce, drain and cut leaves crosswise into 2″ pieces.
3. Cut fish fillets into thin ⅛″ slices.
4. Put chrysanthemum petals in a bowl of cold water to soak 15 minutes. Drain and set aside.

TO COOK: *(cooking time about 10 minutes)*

1. In a large pot bring to a boil chicken broth, water, ginger, and oil.
2. Add lettuce and boil uncovered 1 minute.
3. Add fish and chrysanthemum petals and boil 1 minute.
4. Season with salt and white pepper and serve.
5. To serve: Serve hot at once in soup bowls. Include bits of everything in each serving. This soup cannot sit because the lettuce will wilt and turn yellow and the fish will be over-cooked.
6. Yield: Serves 6.

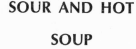

SOUR AND HOT

SOUP

**15 MINUTES
COOKING TIME**

INGREDIENTS:

one 12-oz. can clear chicken broth
2 cans water

—

2 pork chops, cut into thin strips

—

6 Chinese mushrooms, soaked in water until soft
one 8-oz. can sliced bamboo shoots, cut into thin strips
3 pieces fresh beancurd, cut into strips

—

Master sauce:
2 tablespoons cornstarch dissolved in 2 tablespoons water
3 tablespoons white vinegar
1 tablespoon light soy
1 teaspoon red chili oil

—

1 tablespoon sesame oil
2 pieces scallions, cut into 1/8" rings
salt and white pepper to taste

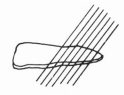

TO PREPARE:

1. Lay chops flat and cut through the meat horizontally so that you have two pieces from each chop. Each should be half as thick as the chop was originally. Cut each piece into thin strips 1/8" wide.

2. Discard stems of softened mushrooms, cut into thin 1/8" strips.

3. Cut bamboo slices into 1/8" strips.

4. Split beancurd in halves crosswise and cut into 1/8" strips.

5. Make master sauce in a cup, set aside.

6. Cut scallions into 1/8" rings.

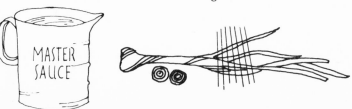

TO COOK: (*cooking time about 15 minutes*)

1. Bring to boil chicken broth and water in a pot.

2. Add pork strips and simmer 2 minutes.

3. Add mushroom, bamboo, and beancurd strips and simmer 5 minutes.

4. Keep soup simmering, add master sauce. Cook, stirring 2 minutes for soup to simmer and thicken.

5. Off heat, add sesame oil and scallions and salt and white pepper to taste. Stir to mix. Serve.

6. To serve: Serve hot in soup bowls. This soup can sit in its covered pot in a warm oven for ½ hour. It must be served hot. Reheat gently, but *do not boil again* as it will overcook the ingredients as well as turning the soup watery.

7. Yield: Serves 6.

Fish and Seafood

INTRODUCTION

Ideally, all seafood used in Chinese cooking should be freshly killed, although most seafood can be kept in the refrigerator for a day or two. But never use frozen seafood for Chinese cooking; once frozen, the meat of seafood becomes soggy and mushy. (The only exception to this is frozen crabmeat if used in small quantities.)

Much of the seafood that is available in China is also available here. And, to a certain extent, substitutions can be made. When a whole fish (head and tail included) is called for in a recipe, you can use sea bass, porgy, flounder or red snapper. Make sure the scales are scraped completely off. Use sole or flounder in dishes that need fillets of fish.

Happily, shellfish is available fresh and in large quantities in most American cities. Included in recipes here will be shrimp (sometimes they must be shelled, but deveining is not necessary unless the recipe calls for splitting open the backs), lobsters, crabs, and clams. Squids, too, will be featured, as the Chinese use them quite often.

If you're planning a multi-course dinner which includes a seafood dish, the dinner should be served immediately after the seafood dish is ready. The less time between when the seafood is cooked and when it is served, the less "fishy" it will taste, and the more the fresh sea flavor will come through.

At a farewell dinner for someone going on a sea voyage, be careful not to turn the fish when it is served—the Chinese regard this as a bad omen, for it means the ship will capsize.

Finally, here are some tips for selecting seafood:

Fish The eyeballs should bulge out, not be dull and sunken. The fish scales should be shiny, the gills bright red, and the flesh firm to touch.

Shrimps Look for stiff, shiny shells, translucent meat. If sold with heads (used in many Chinese dishes), the heads should be firmly attached to the body and not dangling at an angle.

Crabs If parts of the legs or claws are missing, they are no good. The darker colored, heavier crabs with stiff, thick shells have more meat. The crabs available in New York and along the Atlantic seaboard are similar to those found in China.

Clams Choose those with tightly shut shells.

Lobsters Choose the one that is kept alive in a water tank.

Squids The smell will let you know if it is rotten. Or better still, befriend your fishmonger.

BRAISED SEA BASS IN GINGER

AND CHINESE RICE WINE

INGREDIENTS:

one whole 2-lb. sea bass, cleaned and scaled

—

two 2" pieces fresh ginger, crushed flat
6 scallions, each cut in half
3 tablespoons peanut or vegetable oil

—

Master sauce:
2 tablespoons Chinese rice wine
1 cup water
1 tablespoon light soy
1 tablespoon sesame oil
1 teaspoon salt
½ teaspoon sugar

—

1 tablespoon cornstarch dissolved in 1 tablespoon water

—

2 scallions cut into ⅛" rings for garnish

TO PREPARE:

1. Wash sea bass and pat dry.
2. Scrape away skin of ginger, crush to flatten.
3. Cut 6 scallions in half. Cut the other 2 into ⅛" rings to be used as garnish.
4. Make master sauce by combining all ingredients.
5. Dissolve cornstarch in water and set aside.

TO COOK: *(cooking time about 25 minutes)*

1. Heat 3 tablespoons oil in wok over medium flame. Add ginger and scallions, sizzle 1 minute.
2. Add sea bass and sizzle ½ minute each side.
3. Add master sauce, bring to a boil, cover wok, lower flame and simmer gently 20 minutes. Dish up fish carefully on a large platter, cover and keep warm.
5. Discard ginger and scallions from poaching sauce, bring the sauce to a boil and add cornstarch solution, cook, stirring ½ minute for sauce to simmer and thicken.
6. Add scallion rings, stir to mix, pour over fish and serve.
7. To serve: Serve at once, hot. Guests pick meat from the fish, one morsel at a time.
8. Yield: Serves 2 alone or 6 in a 4-course dinner.

POACHED SEA BASS WITH "THREE-RIBBONS"

SWEET AND SOUR SAUCE

**25 MINUTES
COOKING TIME**

INGREDIENTS:

1 whole 2-lb. sea bass, cleaned and scaled
6 cups water
4 thin slices fresh ginger
1 teaspoon salt

—

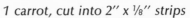

1 carrot, cut into 2" x ⅛" strips
6 scallions, white parts only, cut into strips
½ cup sweet pickles, cut into strips
2 cloves garlic crushed coarsely
3 tablespoons peanut or vegetable oil

—

Sweet and sour sauce:
¼ cup white vinegar
3 tablespoons sugar
2 tablespoons light soy
½ teaspoon salt
1 teaspoon Chinese rice wine or sherry
1 tablespoon cornstarch dissolved in ¾ cup water

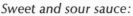

TO PREPARE:

1. Wash sea bass and pat dry.
2. Cut 4 thin slices fresh ginger.
3. Slice carrots lengthwise, then into 2" x ⅛" strips.
4. Cut white parts of scallions into 2" x ⅛" strips.
5. Use any brand of sweet pickles like gherkins; ½ cup cut into 2" x ⅛" strips.
6. Crush garlic.
7. Make sweet and sour sauce by combining all the ingredients in a cup and set aside.

TO COOK: *(cooking time about 25 minutes)*

1. In a pot large enough to hold the fish, bring to boil the water, ginger, and salt.

2. Add sea bass, cover pot, and boil 5 minutes. Turn off heat and let sea bass sit in covered pot for 10 minutes.

3. Meanwhile, heat 3 tablespoons oil in a wok over medium flame. Add garlic and sizzle ½ minute.

4. Add the "three-ribbons"—the carrot, pickle and scallion strips. Stir-fry 3 minutes.

5. Keep mixture simmering, add the sweet and sour sauce from the cup. Bring to a boil and cook, stirring ½ minute for sauce to thicken.

6. To serve: Lift the poached fish from the pot carefully, drain, and place on a large platter. Pour the sauce over it and serve at once hot. This dish cannot sit. Make the sauce while the fish is poaching so that the dish can be served as soon as the fish is cooked.

7. Yield: Serves 2 alone or 6 in a 4-course dinner.

Notes: Vary sugar and vinegar to taste. Other ingredients suitable for "three-ribbons" are Chinese pickled onions, Chinese mushrooms soaked soft, or cucumber, all cut into 2" x ⅛" strips.

20 MINUTES
COOKING TIME

STEAMED SEA BASS WITH CHINESE

MUSHROOMS IN LIGHT SOY

INGREDIENTS:

one whole 1—2 lb. fresh sea bass, cleaned and scaled

—

4 Chinese mushrooms, soaked in water until soft
4 scallions, cut into 2" pieces
8 thin slices fresh ginger, cut into ⅛" strips

—

Master sauce:
2 tablespoons light soy
2 tablespoons peanut or vegetable oil
½ teaspoon salt

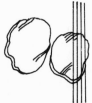

TO PREPARE:

1. Wash sea bass in cold water and pat dry. Put on a heatproof platter which will fit inside your steaming pot. Make 4 shallow gashes at 1" intervals on the top side of the fish facing you.

2. Discard stems and cut softened mushrooms into ⅛" strips.

3. Cut scallions into 2" pieces.

4. Slice fresh ginger thinly, and cut into ⅛" strips.

5. Make master sauce by combining light soy, oil and salt.

TO COOK: (*cooking time about 20 minutes*)

1. Scatter half of the mushrooms, scallions, and ginger strips on top of the fish, and arrange the rest snugly around it. Pour master sauce all over the fish. The dish is ready now to steam.

2. Prepare for steaming (see steaming instruction on page 2). Steam 20 minutes in a steady steam. Serve.

3. To serve: Spoon sauce collected on platter to moisten fish all over, serve at once hot on the steaming platter. Guests pick meat from fish to eat. This dish cannot sit. Time it to finish cooking when you're ready to serve dinner.

4. Yield: Serves 2 alone or 6 in a 4-course dinner.

Notes: Flounder, sole or porgy can also be used for this dish.

20 MINUTES
COOKING TIME

RED-COOKED RED SNAPPER

WITH CHINESE MUSHROOMS

INGREDIENTS:

one whole 2-lb. red snapper, cleaned and scaled
2 tablespoons flour for coating
3 tablespoons peanut or vegetable oil

—

6 scallions, cut into 2" pieces
6 Chinese mushrooms, soaked in water until soft
1 tablespoon peanut or vegetable oil
1 clove garlic, crushed

—

Master sauce:
¼ cup dark soy
1 tablespoon cornstarch dissolved in 1 cup water
1 tablespoon Chinese rice wine or sherry
1 teaspoon sugar
½ teaspoon salt

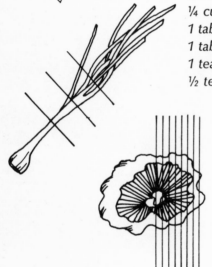

TO PREPARE:

1. Wash the fish and pat dry. Roll in flour to coat thinly, shake off excess. Set aside.

2. Cut scallions into 2" pieces.

3. Discard stems and cut softened mushrooms into ⅛" strips.

4. Crush garlic.

5. Make master sauce in a cup by combining all the ingredients.

TO COOK: *(cooking time about 20 minutes)*

1. Heat 3 tablespoons oil in wok over medium flame. Add fish and shallow-fry 3 minutes each side until light brown. Carefully transfer fish to a platter, set aside.

2. Discard oil from wok, rinse in hot water, pat dry. Heat 1 tablespoon oil in wok over medium flame, add garlic and sizzle a few seconds, add scallions and mushrooms, stir-fry 1 minute.

3. Add master sauce and bring to a boil to thicken.

4. Place fish in sauce, arrange mushrooms and scallions on top and cover wok to braise gently 10 minutes. Serve.

5. To serve: Place fish carefully on a large platter and pour sauce on top, serve at once hot. Guests take meat from the fish one morsel at a time.

6. Yield: Serves 2 alone or 6 in a 4-course dinner.

Notes: Other suitable fish are sea bass and porgy.

STIR-FRIED FLOUNDER FILLETS

WITH SCALLIONS

INGREDIENTS:

1 lb. flounder fillets
1 tablespoon cornstarch
1 tablespoon light soy
1 tablespoon Chinese rice wine or sherry
¼ teaspoon salt
dash white pepper

—

4 tablespoons peanut or vegetable oil
4 thin slices fresh ginger
3 scallions, cut into 2″ strips

—

Master sauce:
1 tablespoon light soy
2 tablespoons water
½ teaspoon sugar
1 teaspoon sesame oil

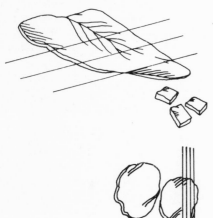

TO PREPARE:

1. Cut fish into 1″ cubes. Put in a bowl and add to it cornstarch, light soy, wine, salt, and white pepper. Mix well and marinate 1 hour.

2. Cut 4 thin slices fresh ginger. Cut each slice into ⅛″ strips.

3. Cut scallions into 2″ lengths.

4. Make the master sauce by combining all ingredients in a cup.

TO COOK: *(cooking time about 5 minutes)*

1. Heat 4 tablespoons oil in a wok over medium-high flame. Add scallions and ginger, sizzle ½ minute.

2. Add marinated fish and stir-fry 4 minutes. Make sure the fish is sizzling all the time, otherwise the fish will ooze juice.

3. Keeping the fish at a sizzle, add the master sauce from the cup. Stir-fry ½ minute for sauce to simmer and thicken. Serve.

4. To serve: Dish up in a plate and serve hot at once. This dish cannot sit as it will lose its *wok hay* and become fishy.

5. Yield: Serves 2 if the only course, or 6 in a 4-course dinner.

Notes: You may also use fillets of sole, pike or sea bass.

STIR-FRIED SHRIMPS AND CAULIFLOWER
IN LIGHT SOY

**7 MINUTES
COOKING TIME**

INGREDIENTS:

1 lb. small shrimps, shelled
1 tablespoon light soy
1 tablespoon Chinese rice wine or sherry
1 teaspoon cornstarch
1 teaspoon sesame oil
dash white pepper
¼ teaspoon salt
—

½ lb. cauliflower sprigs
6 cups water
1 teaspoon salt
—

2 tablespoons peanut or vegetable oil
2 thin slices fresh ginger, cut into ⅛" strips
2 scallions, cut into 1" lengths
—

Master sauce:
1 teaspoon cornstarch dissolved in ¼ cup water
2 tablespoons light soy
1 teaspoon sesame oil

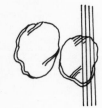

TO PREPARE:

1. Shell the shrimps. Put them in a bowl and add light soy, wine, cornstarch, sesame oil, pepper and salt. Mix well and marinate for 1 hour.

2. Cut cauliflower into small bite-size sprays—use the flower sprigs only. Bring 6 cups water and salt to the boil in a pot, add cauliflower sprigs and boil uncovered 2 minutes. Drain and reserve.

3. Slice fresh ginger, then cut into ⅛" strips. Cut scallions into 1" lengths.

4. Make the master sauce by combining all ingredients in a cup.

TO COOK: *(cooking time about 7 minutes)*

1. Heat 2 tablespoons oil in the wok over medium-high flame. Add ginger and scallions and sizzle ½ minute.

2. Add shrimps and stir-fry, sizzling, 3 minutes. Keep stirring and turning to cook evenly.

3. Add cauliflower and stir-fry 2 minutes to mix and heat through.

4. Adjust flame to medium, keep mixture simmering, add master sauce. Cook, stirring 1 minute for sauce to simmer and thicken. Serve.

5. To serve: Dish up on a large plate and serve hot at once.

6. Yield: Serves 2 alone or 6 in a 4-course dinner.

STIR-FRIED SHRIMPS

IN LOBSTER SAUCE

**10 MINUTES
COOKING TIME**

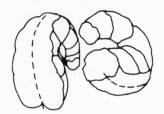

INGREDIENTS:

    1 lb. medium raw shrimps, shelled
    1 tablespoon Chinese rice wine or sherry
    1 teaspoon cornstarch

    —

    2 tablespoons peanut or vegetable oil

    —

    1 tablespoon peanut or vegetable oil
    4 cloves garlic, chopped fine
    1 tablespoon fermented black beans, chopped coarsely

    —

    ¼ lb. lean pork (about 1 pork chop), ground

    —

    Master sauce:
    1 tablespoon cornstarch dissolved in ¾ cup water
    2 tablespoons light soy
    ½ teaspoon sugar
    ¼ teaspoon salt

    —

    2 eggs, beaten

TO PREPARE:

    1. Shell the shrimps. Make an ⅛″ slit down the back and devein. Pat dry. Half an hour before cooking, dissolve cornstarch in 1 tablespoon Chinese wine or sherry and marinate shrimp in wine-cornstarch mixture.

    2. Chop garlic fine, and black beans coarsely.

    3. Chop or grind pork if butcher has not done so.

    4. Make the master sauce by combining all ingredients in a cup.

    5. Beat eggs lightly to mix, set aside.

TO COOK: *(cooking time about 10 minutes)*

    1. Heat 2 tablespoons oil in wok over high flame. Add shrimps and stir-fry sizzling 4 minutes. Dish up on a plate and set aside.

2. In the same wok over high flame, heat 1 tablespoon oil, then add garlic and black beans and sizzle ½ minute.

3. Add ground pork and stir-fry 2 minutes to cook. Then add cooked shrimps from plate, stir to mix.

4. Keep mixture simmering, add the master sauce and cook stirring 1 minute for sauce to simmer and thicken.

5. Stir in the beaten eggs, and keep stirring for ½ minute for eggs to cook slightly. Serve.

6. To serve: Dish up in a large plate and serve very hot. This dish cannot sit as the sauce will lose its *wok hay* (wok flavor).

7. Yield: Serves 2 alone or 6 in a 4-course dinner.

Notes: During the cooking, make sure the pork and shrimps are simmering before adding the master sauce. Then bring to a simmer to thicken. Stir in the eggs continuously till the mixture is just cooked.

This master sauce is called "lobster sauce" because lobster is often cooked in a similar sauce; the name of that dish is "Lobster Cantonese." To make Lobster Cantonese, substitute a 2 lb. lobster cut into 2" pieces for the shrimp (see steamed lobster dish on page 62 for cutting instructions) and follow the recipe exactly as the one above.

**5 MINUTES
COOKING TIME**

STIR-FRIED SHRIMPS SZECHUAN

IN HOT BROWN BEAN SAUCE

INGREDIENTS:

3 tablespoons peanut or vegetable oil
6 cloves garlic, crushed and chopped fine
4 scallions, cut into 2" lengths
½ teaspoon dry red chili pepper, crushed coarsely
1 lb. raw medium shrimps, shelled
—

Hot sauce:
1 tablespoon hot brown bean sauce (dow barn jeung)
2 tablespoons tomato ketchup
1 teaspoon Chinese rice wine or sherry
2 tablespoons water
½ teaspoon sugar
½ teaspoon salt

TO PREPARE:

1. Crush and chop garlic fine; cut scallions into 2" pieces.

2. Crush dry red chili pepper coarsely: or you can use any bottled brand of crushed red pepper flakes.

3. Shell shrimp, but do not remove tail shell.

4. Make the hot sauce by combining all the ingredients in a cup.

TO COOK: *(cooking time about 5 minutes)*

1. Heat 3 tablespoons oil in wok over high flame. Add garlic, scallions, and red pepper, sizzle 1 minute.

2. Add shrimps and stir-fry sizzling 2 minutes.

3. Add the hot sauce and stir-fry 2 minutes. Most of the sauce is boiled away leaving enough to coat the shrimps. Serve.

4. To serve: Dish up on a plate and serve hot at once to taste the fiery wok flavor. This dish cannot sit as the garlicky Szechuan flavor will be lost.

5. Yield: Serves 2 if the only course, or 6 in a 4-course dinner.

SHALLOW-FRIED SHRIMPS

IN KETCHUP SAUCE

8 MINUTES
COOKING TIME

INGREDIENTS:

1 lb. fresh raw shrimp
1 tablespoon light soy
1 tablespoon Chinese rice wine or sherry
—

3 tablespoons peanut or vegetable oil
4 scallions, cut into 2" pieces
—

Ketchup sauce:
4 tablespoons tomato ketchup
1 teaspoon cornstarch dissolved in 2 tablespoons water
½ teaspoon salt

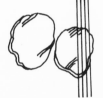

TO PREPARE:

1. Wash shrimps and pat dry. Leave shells on. Marinate with light soy and wine for ½ hour.
2. Cut scallions into 2" pieces.
3. Make ketchup sauce by combining all the ingredients in a cup.

TO COOK: *(cooking time about 8 minutes)*

1. Heat 3 tablespoons oil in wok over high flame. Add scallions and sizzle ½ minute.
2. Add shrimps and stir-fry sizzling 5 minutes. Shells should be slightly singed.
3. Turn flame to medium, add ketchup sauce, and cook stirring ½ minute for sauce to simmer and thicken. Serve.
4. To serve: Dish up on a plate and serve very hot. Guests discard shells when they eat. The Chinese can spit the shells out gracefully after savoring all the sauce on the shells first.
5. Yield: Serves 2 alone or 6 in a 4-course dinner.

Notes: Keep the wok very hot when stir-frying the shrimps so that the juice is sealed in. If shrimps are sold with heads on, keep the heads; the Chinese consider the head the best part of the shrimp.

20 MINUTES
COOKING TIME

STEAMED LOBSTER

IN BLACK BEAN SAUCE

INGREDIENTS:

1 live lobster, 1½—2 lbs.

—

Master sauce:
2 tablespoons fermented black beans, chopped coarsely
4 cloves garlic, chopped coarsely
2 thin slices fresh ginger, chopped fine
2 tablespoons peanut or vegetable oil
1 tablespoon dark soy
1 tablespoon Chinese rice wine or sherry
1 teaspoon sesame oil
½ teaspoon sugar
½ teaspoon salt

MASTER
SAUCE

TO PREPARE:

1. Ask your fishmonger to chop the lobster in 2″ pieces including the head. Or do it yourself as follows: Kill lobster by chopping off the head at the first joint of the shell. Chop off claws, crush, and cut claws into 2″ pieces. Chop away and discard eyes and antennae. Discard also gills and stomach sac. Chop head into 2 pieces. For the body, chop and discard legs except for the meaty part next to the body. Split body lengthwise in halves, chop each half into 2″ pieces.

2. Chop black beans, garlic and ginger.

3. Make the master sauce by combining all the ingredients in a cup.

62

TO COOK: *(cooking time about 20 minutes)*

1. Prepare for steaming. (See steaming instructions on page 2.)

2. Arrange lobster pieces in a heatproof pie dish or plate.

3. Pour the master sauce all over the meat.

4. Steam 20 minutes. Serve.

5. To serve: Serve very hot in the steaming plate. Do not reheat or let lobster sit in pot to keep warm, for the meat will get all soggy.

6. Yield: Serves 2 alone or 6 in a 4-course dinner.

Notes: This is a very simple and tasty way of preparing a lobster. All the juices are collected in the plate while steaming, nothing is lost in cooking. The other good way of preparing a lobster is Lobster Cantonese on pages 58–59.

**15 MINUTES
COOKING TIME**

STIR-FRIED CRABS WITH SCALLIONS

AND GINGER

INGREDIENTS:

4 live crabs, cleaned and each cut into 6 pieces

—

4 tablespoons peanut or vegetable oil
6 scallions, cut into 2" lengths
6 thin slices fresh ginger, cut into ⅛" strips

—

Master sauce:
3 tablespoons light soy
1 tablespoon cornstarch dissolved in 1 tablespoon water
¼ teaspoon salt
dash white pepper

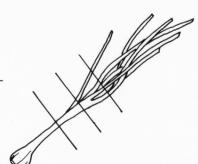

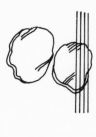

TO PREPARE:

1. Lay the crab on the table with legs on top. Cut into 2 equal halves. For each half separate the shell from the body. Rinse shell in water, being careful to reserve the yellow matter. Set aside. Wash the halved body and discard hairy matter. Cut in 2 pieces. Repeat for the other half. Each crab yields 4 meaty pieces and 2 shell pieces.

2. Cut scallions into 2" lengths.

3. Cut thin slices fresh ginger into ⅛" strips.

4. Make master sauce in a cup by combining all the ingredients in a cup.

TO COOK: *(cooking time about 15 minutes)*

1. Heat 4 tablespoons oil in wok over high flame. Add scallions and ginger, sizzle ½ minute.

2. Add crab pieces and stir-fry 2 minutes. Cover wok, lower flame to medium and sizzle 10 minutes. Crabs should be just cooked.

3. Add master sauce to the crabs, and cook stirring 1 minute for sauce to simmer and thicken. Serve.

4. To serve: Dish up in a large platter and serve hot at once to enjoy the fresh wok flavor. Chinese usually serve this at the beginning of the meal so that it is piping hot, then the table is cleared of crab shells and the meal continues. The crabs are picked up with the chopsticks, you suck on the sauce and the meat, and spit out the shells.

5. Yield: Serves 2 alone or 6 in a 4-course dinner.

10 MINUTES
COOKING TIME

STIR-FRIED CLAMS

IN HOISIN SAUCE

INGREDIENTS:

2 dozen fresh clams in shells

—

2 tablespoons peanut or vegetable oil
2 cloves garlic

—

Master sauce:
1 teaspoon cornstarch dissolved in ¼ cup water
3 tablespoons hoisin *sauce*
salt to taste

TO PREPARE:

1. Scrub and soak clams in cold water for 2 hours. When ready to cook drain and pat dry.

2. Crush 2 cloves garlic.

3. Make the master sauce by combining all the ingredients in a cup.

TO COOK: *(cooking time about 10 minutes)*

1. Heat 2 tablespoons oil in wok over high flame. Add garlic and sizzle ½ minute.

2. Add clams and stir-fry 2 minutes. Cover wok and sizzle 5 minutes or until all the shells are open.

3. Add master sauce and cook stirring ½ minute for sauce to simmer and thicken. Serve.

4. To serve: Dish up in a large platter and serve hot at once. This dish cannot sit or the sauce will turn gluey and lose its *wok hay.*

5. Yield: Serves 2 alone or 6 in a 4-course dinner.

Notes: This is a dish that the Chinese often serve during the New Year. When the clams burst open, it means business is blooming and the new year will be full of prosperity.

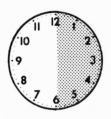

30 MINUTES
COOKING TIME

BRAISED SQUIDS AND HARD-BOILED EGGS

IN DARK SOY

INGREDIENTS:

>   2 lbs. medium fresh squids, boned and cleaned
>   2 thin slices fresh ginger
>   2 tablespoons peanut or vegetable oil
>   —
>   *Master sauce:*
>   ½ cup dark soy
>   1 cup water
>   2 whole star anise
>   1 teaspoon sugar
>   ½ teaspoon salt
>   —
>   2 eggs, hard-boiled

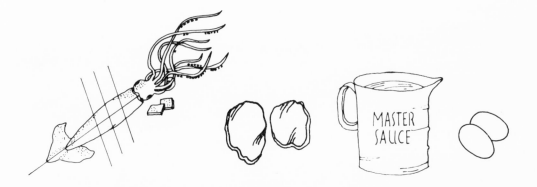

TO PREPARE:

   1. Wash the cleaned squids and pat dry. Cut into 2″ pieces.

   2. Cut 2 thin slices fresh ginger.

   3. Make the master sauce by combining all the ingredients in a cup.

   4. Hard boil the eggs and shell. Set aside.

TO COOK: *(cooking time about 30 minutes)*

1. Heat 2 tablespoons oil in a heavy casserole over medium flame. Add ginger slices. When oil sizzles add the squid. Stir-fry ½ minute.

2. Add master sauce. Bring to the boil.

3. Lower flame, cover pot, and simmer gently 20 minutes.

4. Add the shelled hard-boiled eggs and simmer 10 minutes. This dish is ready now to serve hot or at room temperature.

5. To serve: Cut each egg into 4 sections. Place squid on a large plate and surround it with the egg sections. Pour the sauce over all. This dish can sit for hours in the pot, and be reheated when needed. Or it can be prepared a day or two in advance and served cold from the refrigerator.

6. Yield: Serves 2 alone or 6 in a 4-course dinner.

Notes: This is a good cocktail dish too.

**8 MINUTES
COOKING TIME**

STIR-FRIED SQUIDS WITH

PICKLED MUSTARD GREEN

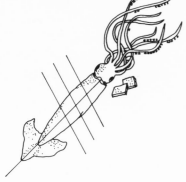

INGREDIENTS:

1 lb. fresh medium size squids, cleaned and boned
1 tablespoon Chinese rice wine or sherry
2 tablespoons light soy

—

3 tablespoons peanut or vegetable oil
2 thin slices fresh ginger, chopped coarsely
1 whole pickled mustard green

—

Master sauce:
1 teaspoon cornstarch dissolved in ¼ cup water
1 tablespoon light soy
½ teaspoon sugar

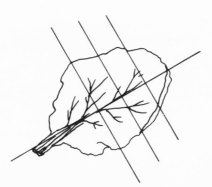

TO PREPARE:

    1. Wash cleaned squids and pat dry. Score diamond pattern on one side of the skin. Cut into 1" pieces.

    2. Slice ginger and chop coarsely.

    3. Separate stalks and wash pickled mustard green. Cut stalks in half, lengthwise; then cut into 2" pieces.

    4. Make master sauce by combining all the ingredients in a cup.

TO COOK: *(cooking time about 8 minutes)*

1. Toss squids with rice wine and light soy, marinate 1 minute.

2. Heat 3 tablespoons oil in wok over high flame, add chopped ginger and sizzle ½ minute.

3. Add squids and stir-fry at a sizzle 3 minutes.

4. Add mustard green and stir-fry 2 minutes.

5. Add master sauce and cook stirring ½ minute for sauce to simmer and thicken. Serve.

6. To serve: Dish up in a plate and serve hot at once to taste the wok flavor.

7. Yield: Serves 2 alone or 6 in a 4-course dinner.

Notes: Pickled mustard green, sold by the piece in a Chinese grocery store, is very sour and salty, so you must adjust sugar and salt to taste.

Beef and Pork

INTRODUCTION

In China, vegetable and fish dishes are more popular than meat dishes. Among the meats, the Chinese prefer chicken and pork to beef and duck.

Dark red meat dripping with blood does not appeal to most Chinese. Beef especially, is considered a very "smelly" meat and "heating" to the body, not at all a civilized dish! (And lambs are so smelly that only the barbaric Mongols eat them!)

Through the years, beef has been grudgingly accepted because of its food value. Also, in China, it is much less expensive than pork. The Chinese consume great quantities of very fat pork (fay jew yoke), so that beef with its leaner meat is a change.

In the recipes that follow, only a few cuts of meat are suggested; this is for your shopping convenience. For beef dishes, flank steak and ground round are used. For pork, mainly pork chops, ground or sliced are used, plus the popular spare ribs, roast pork, tenderloin, and pigs' feet.

Most meat dishes use the stir-fry method of cooking. In this method, the thinly sliced meat is marinated with a basic mixture of soy, cornstarch, rice wine, and sugar just before being put in the sizzling wok. This marinade serves as a tenderizing binder for the meat. Get into the habit of mixing the meat briefly with the marinade and you're halfway toward a perfect dish.

When the meat is accompanied by other ingredients, a vegetable for example, either the meat or the vegetable is cooked first, transferred to a side plate, and then the next ingredient is cooked. A final step is to toss everything back into the wok for a final mix before serving. So get used to the idea of doing separate little dishes and then one final toss for the finished entree.

The Chinese are used to eating just-done pork and, by Western standards, well-done beef. Here, in the United States, it is the reverse. Everybody cooks pork for hours, for fear of catching a parasitic disease, but eats beef as rare as possible.

Do remember that in Chinese cooking, the meat is always sliced very thinly, and the wok is always sizzling hot, so you need to cook the meat only very briefly before it is cooked through—and that applies to pork especially. (In stir-fry pork dishes, the pork is either ground finely or sliced very thin.) Drink some brandy for the lingering germs if you're the worrying type. The Chinese believe brandy will kill any larvae or bacteria!

BRAISED BONELESS PORK

TENDERLOIN SHANGHAI

INGREDIENTS:

2—3 lbs. boneless pork tenderloin in one piece

—

Master sauce:
½ cup oyster sauce
1 cup water
2 tablespoons dark soy
2 tablespoons Chinese rice wine or sherry
½ teaspoon salt

—

4 eggs
2 tablespoons peanut or vegetable oil

TO PREPARE:

1. Make 4 shallow gashes on top side of pork.

2. Make master sauce by combining all the ingredients in a cup.

TO COOK: *(cooking time about 2 hours)*

1. In a heavy casserole large enough to hold the piece of pork, bring the master sauce to a boil.

2. Add the pork, cover pot and lower flame. Simmer for 2 hours. Turn pork every half hour to prevent sticking.

3. Meanwhile, fry each egg separately in oil till the yolks are hard and both sides are golden brown. Reserve.

4. Add the eggs to the pork during the last 10 minutes of braising. Serve.

5. To serve: Dish up the pork and cut into ¼" slices. Place the eggs on a large platter, arrange the pork slices on top, pour the sauce over and serve hot. This dish can sit in its pot for 1—2 hours, but in that case, do not slice the meat. When needed, reheat, slice the meat, and serve.

6. Yield: Serves 4 alone or 6 in a 4-course dinner.

Notes: This is a simple dish to prepare and very nourishing. It is served often in family dinners in China as the sauce is delicious with the rice.

1 HOUR
COOKING TIME

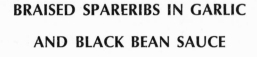

BRAISED SPARERIBS IN GARLIC

AND BLACK BEAN SAUCE

INGREDIENTS:

1 lb. spareribs, cut into 2" x 1" pieces

2 tablespoons peanut or vegetable oil
4 cloves garlic, crushed and chopped fine
3 tablespoons fermented black beans, chopped coarsely

—

Master sauce:
1 cup water
1 tablespoon dark soy
1 teaspoon sugar
¼ teaspoon salt

TO PREPARE:

1. Ask your butcher to cut spareribs into 2" x 1" pieces. Or chop it up yourself with a sharp heavy knife like a cleaver.

2. Crush garlic and chop fine. Chop black beans coarsely.

3. Make master sauce by combining all the ingredients in a cup.

TO COOK: *(cooking time about 1 hour)*

1. Heat 2 tablespoons oil in a heavy casserole over medium flame. Add garlic and black beans, stir-fry 1 minute.

2. Add spareribs and stir-fry 1 minute.

3. Add master sauce, bring to a boil. Cover pot, lower flame and simmer 1 hour. Stir every 15 minutes to prevent sticking. Serve.

4. To serve: Pour the spareribs and the sauce in a large deep platter and serve hot. This dish can sit in its pot for hours. Reheat to serve.

5. Yield: Serves 2 alone or 6 in a 4-course dinner.

**2 HOURS
COOKING TIME**

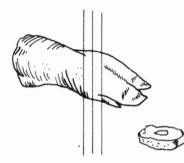

BRAISED PIGS' FEET IN DARK SOY

ON BED OF SPINACH

INGREDIENTS:

3 pigs' feet, cut into 1" pieces

—

½ cup dark soy
2 cups water
1 whole star anise
1 tablespoon sugar
1 tablespoon Chinese rice wine or sherry
2 thin slices fresh ginger

—

1 lb. fresh spinach
6 cups water
1 teaspoon salt

TO PREPARE:

1. Ask the butcher to cut pigs' feet into 1" pieces, or cut them yourself with a sharp heavy knife.
2. Cut 2 slices fresh ginger.
3. Wash spinach and drain.

TO COOK: *(cooking time about 2 hours)*

1. In a large, heavy pot bring to boil the dark soy, water, star anise, sugar, wine, and ginger.
2. Add pigs' feet and boil uncovered 10 minutes. Skim off any scum floating on surface.
3. Lower flame, cover pot, and simmer for 2 hours. Stir the meat every ½ hour to prevent sticking. Make sure there's always about 1—2 cups liquid in the pot. Add water if necessary.
4. Meanwhile, bring to boil in another pot 6 cups water and salt. Add the spinach and boil 1 minute. Drain and keep warm.
5. To serve: Spread the spinach on a large platter, place the pigs' feet on top, and pour the sauce over them. Serve very hot. The pigs' feet can be cooked the day before, and reheated to serve.
6. Yield: Serves 4 alone or 6 in a 4-course dinner.

BRAISED PORK LION HEADS

WITH CHINESE CELERY CABBAGE

50 MINUTES
COOKING TIME

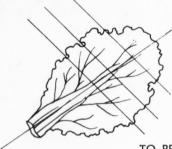

INGREDIENTS:

1 lb. ground pork (ask your butcher to grind it for you)

Pork marinade:
2 scallions, finely chopped
1 teaspoon finely chopped fresh ginger
1 tablespoon Chinese rice wine or sherry
3 tablespoons light soy
1 egg, beaten
1 tablespoon cornstarch
½ teaspoon salt

*Batter: 2 tablespoons cornstarch dissolved in 2 table-
spoons water*

3 tablespoons peanut or vegetable oil

1 whole celery cabbage, cut into 2" pieces

½ cup clear chicken broth
1 tablespoon dark soy
1 teaspoon sugar
1 teaspoon salt

TO PREPARE:

1. Chop scallions and ginger, finely. Make pork marinade by combining all the ingredients in a bowl. Add ground pork and mix well. Divide pork into 10 portions and shape into balls.

2. Make a batter with the cornstarch and water.

3. Wash and separate stalks of celery cabbage. Halve lengthwise, then cut into 2" pieces.

TO COOK: *(cooking time about 50 minutes)*

1. Heat 3 tablespoons oil in wok over medium flame. Coat pork balls with batter, then put them in the wok to fry. Fry 2 minutes, turning, so that all sides are golden brown. Drain and set aside. These are the "lion heads."

2. Arrange celery cabbage (these are the "lions' manes") at the bottom of a heavy casserole. Place the lion heads on top.

3. Mix together chicken broth, dark soy, sugar, and salt and pour this into the casserole. Bring to a boil.

4. Cover pot, reduce flame and simmer 45 minutes. Serve.

5. To serve: Serve piping hot from the casserole pot. This dish can sit for hours or overnight, in fact, the flavor seems to improve with sitting. Reheat to serve.

6. Yield: Serves 4 alone or 6 in a 4-course dinner.

30 MINUTES
COOKING TIME

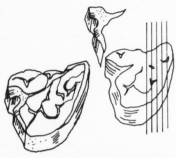

MASTER
SAUCE

STEAMED PORK SLICES WITH

PICKLED KOHLRABI HEADS

INGREDIENTS:

4 pork chops, each about ¾'' thick, cut in ⅛'' slices

—

Master sauce:
1 teaspoon cornstarch dissolved in ½ cup water
1 tablespoon peanut or vegetable oil
1 tablespoon light soy
1 teaspoon sugar

—

2 pieces pickled kohlrabi, cut into ⅛'' slices

TO PREPARE:

1. Cut away and discard the bones of each pork chop. Trim excess fat. Lay chop flat on board and slice ⅛'' thick.

2. Wash kohlrabi heads in water. (There are about 6 heads in each can, the rest keep forever in a sealed jar in the refrigerator.) Cut each head into very thin, ⅛'' slices.

3. Make master sauce by combining all ingredients in a cup.

TO COOK: (cooking time about 30 minutes)

1. Prepare for steaming according to steaming instructions on page 2.

2. Use a heatproof pie plate for steaming. Place the pork slices on the plate, add master sauce, and mix well.

3. Stir in the kohlrabi head slices. This dish is now ready to steam.

4. Steam 25 minutes. Serve.

5. To serve: Transfer the pork and sauce to a platter and serve hot.

6. Yield: Serves 2 alone or 6 in a 4-course dinner.

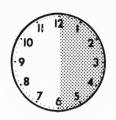

30 MINUTES
COOKING TIME

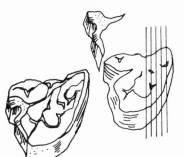

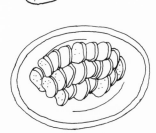

STEAMED LEAN PORK SERVED COLD

SZECHUAN STYLE

INGREDIENTS:

4 very lean pork chops about ¾" thick

—

Szechuan sauce:
4 tablespoons white vinegar
3 tablespoons fish sauce (See page 15 on bottled fish sauce.)
4 cloves garlic, chopped fine
2 tablespoons sesame oil
1 teaspoon red chili oil or to taste
½ teaspoon sugar
salt to taste

TO PREPARE:

1. Trim and discard bone on pork chops. Then trim away any fat or gristle. The pork should be just lean meat.

2. Chop garlic finely.

TO COOK: *(cooking time about 30 minutes)*

1. Prepare for steaming according to steaming instruction on page 2. Put pork chops on a heatproof plate and steam 20 minutes.

2. Lift out and cool, then chill in the refrigerator for use later.

3. Meanwhile, make the Szechuan sauce by combining all the ingredients in a bowl. Cover and chill.

4. To serve: Lay chops flat on board, slice into very thin ⅛" pieces. Arrange in overlapping circles on a platter. Pour the Szechuan sauce over them and serve cold. The pork can be cooked in advance and chilled. It is then sliced when ready to serve. Vary the amount of vinegar and red chili oil to individual taste.

5. Yield: Serves 2 alone or 6 in a 4-course dinner.

Notes: If fish sauce is not available, substitute light soy.

**10 MINUTES
COOKING TIME**

STIR-FRIED SPICY DICED PORK

SZECHUAN

INGREDIENTS:

2 pork chops, cut into ¼" dices
4 cloves garlic, crushed and chopped fine
2 tablespoons peanut or vegetable oil
—
15 dried shrimp, soaked in water until soft
2 green peppers, cut into ¼" dice
6 Chinese mushrooms, soaked in water until soft
—

Master sauce:
1 tablespoon hot brown bean sauce
2 tablespoons hoisin sauce
2 tablespoons dark soy
2 tablespoons water

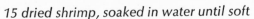

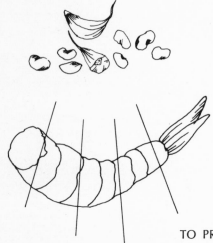
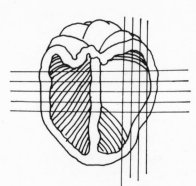

TO PREPARE:

1. Cut and discard bones of pork chops. Split chops in half horizontally. Cut into ¼" strips, then ¼" dice.

2. Crush garlic and chop fine.

3. Cut softened dried shrimp into ¼" dice.

4. Remove seeds from green peppers and cut into ¼" dice.

5. Discard stems and cut softened mushrooms into ¼" dice.

6. Make master sauce by combining all ingredients in a cup.

TO COOK: *(cooking time about 10 minutes)*

1. Heat 2 tablespoons oil in wok over medium flame. Add garlic and sizzle ½ minute.

2. Add diced pork and stir-fry 3 minutes.

3. Add diced shrimp, green peppers and mushrooms, and stir-fry 2 minutes.

4. Pour master sauce into the sizzling mixture and cook, stirring 2 minutes for sauce to simmer and thicken. Serve.

5. To serve: Can be served hot or cold or warm. This is a very spicy dish, and is taken in small amounts over rice. This dish can be made in advance and kept in the refrigerator. A Chinese family will make a large quantity at one time and reheat a small amount to serve when wanted. This is more a side dish than a main course.

6. Yield: Serves 6 in a 4-course dinner.

HOME-MADE ROAST PORK
WITH HOISIN SAUCE

INGREDIENTS:

2 lbs. boneless pork tenderloin in one piece

—

Pork marinade:
4 tablespoons hoisin sauce
2 tablespoons Chinese rice wine or sherry
4 tablespoons dark soy
2 tablespoons honey
1 teaspoon salt
½ teaspoon garlic, chopped fine
4 thin slices fresh ginger, chopped fine

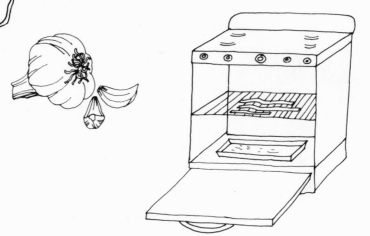

TO PREPARE:

1. Cut pork tenderloin lengthwise into 3 or 4 long strips about 1½" in diameter. Keep the strips fairly narrow so that they can be cooked through evenly.

2. Chop garlic and ginger, finely. Make pork marinade by combining all the ingredients in a cup.

3. Place the pork strips in a shallow pan, pour the marinade over them. Marinate 3—4 hours or overnight in the refrigerator. Baste pork to marinate thoroughly.

TO COOK: *(cooking time about 1 hour)*

1. Prepare the oven for roasting: The pork strips are placed directly on the top rack of the oven, and roasted at high heat. To catch the drippings, remove the lower oven rack, half-fill a large roasting pan with water and place beneath the pork to catch the fat drippings and to prevent smoking *or* roast on a cookie sheet, although the flavor is better with direct roasting on an open rack.

2. Preheat the oven to 375° F.

3. Place pork strips directly on top oven rack and roast 20 minutes. Baste with marinade left over from marinating the pork and roast 10 minutes more.

4. Turn meat over and roast 20 minutes. Baste and roast another 10 minutes. The pork should be very brown.

5. To serve: Slice pork thinly and serve hot, warm, or cold.

6. Yield: Serves 4 alone or 6 in a 4-course dinner.

Notes: Left-over roast pork can be wrapped and stored in the refrigerator for up to 2 weeks. Use it in any dishes calling for roast pork as an ingredient, or in place of cooked ham in such dishes as fried rice, or beancurd dishes.

BRAISED BEEF WITH STAR ANISE

IN DARK SOY

**2 HOURS
COOKING TIME**

INGREDIENTS:

    2 lbs. stewing beef (chuck or a similar cut) in one piece
    2 tablespoons peanut or vegetable oil
    4 thin slices fresh ginger
    —
    Master sauce:
    1 cup dark soy
    1 tablespoon Chinese rice wine or sherry
    3 cups water
    1 tablespoon sugar
    4 whole star anise

TO PREPARE:

    1. Wash beef and pat dry.

    2. Cut 4 thin slices fresh ginger.

    3. Make master sauce by combining all the ingredients in a cup.

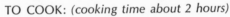

TO COOK: *(cooking time about 2 hours)*

    1. In a heavy casserole large enough to hold the piece of beef, heat 2 tablespoons oil over medium flame. Add ginger and sizzle ½ minute.

    2. Add beef and brown 1 minute each side.

    3. Add master sauce, bring to a boil uncovered.

    4. Reduce flame to low, cover pot and simmer 2 hours. Turn beef over every half hour to prevent sticking and to braise evenly. Make sure there are always about 2 cups liquid in the pot, add more water if necessary.

    5. To serve: Serve either hot, cold, or at room temperature. When ready to serve, lift out beef, cut into ⅛″ thick slices, arrange on a platter and pour the sauce over it. This dish improves with sitting. Reheat to serve hot; or serve cold as a summer meal, or for cocktail tidbits.

    6. Yield: Serves 4 alone or 6 in a 4-course dinner.

8 MINUTES
COOKING TIME

STEAMED GROUND BEEF

WITH CHOPPED SCALLIONS

INGREDIENTS:

1 lb. ground beef
3 scallions, chopped fine
2 teaspoons cornstarch dissolved in ¼ cup water
2 tablespoons light soy
1 tablespoon peanut or vegetable oil
1 teaspoon Chinese rice wine or sherry
1 teaspoon sugar
½ teaspoon salt
dash white pepper

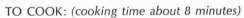

TO PREPARE:

1. Chop scallions.

2. Put the ground beef in a large bowl and add all the other ingredients. Mix thoroughly with a wooden spoon.

3. Spread mixture on an 8″ pie plate or heatproof platter. Meat should be 1–2″ deep. This dish is now ready to steam.

TO COOK: *(cooking time about 8 minutes)*

1. Prepare for steaming according to steaming instructions on page 2.

2. Put beef into steaming pot and steam 8 minutes in a very gentle steam. Serve.

3. To serve: Serve hot at once in its steaming plate. This dish cannot sit or the beef will be overcooked. Time it so that the beef dish is ready when dinner is served. Use a very gentle steam so that the beef comes out rare and smooth.

4. Yield: Serves 2 alone or 6 in a 4-course dinner.

Notes: This dish is served regularly in a Chinese home. It is suitable for young children, as the meat and sauce go well with rice, and there's no bone. The dish is steamed over rice to economize on fuel.

**15 MINUTES
COOKING TIME**

STIR-FRIED GROUND BEEF

WITH GREEN BEANS

INGREDIENTS:

> 1 lb. fresh green beans
> 2 tablespoons peanut or vegetable oil
> 2 thin slices fresh ginger
> ½ teaspoon salt
>
> —
>
> ½ lb. ground beef
> 1 tablespoon peanut or vegetable oil
> 1 clove garlic, crushed
>
> —
>
> Beef sauce:
> 2 tablespoons cornstarch dissolved in ¼ cup water
> 2 tablespoons dark soy
> 1 teaspoon Chinese rice wine or sherry
> 1 teaspoon sugar
> ½ teaspoon salt

TO PREPARE:

1. Destring green beans; wash, dry, and cut into 2" lengths.
2. Cut 2 thin slices fresh ginger.
3. Crush garlic.
4. Make beef sauce by combining all the ingredients in a cup.

TO COOK: *(cooking time about 15 minutes)*

1. Heat 2 tablespoons oil in wok over medium flame. Add ginger and sizzle ½ minute.

2. Add green beans and salt and stir-fry 2 minutes. Cover wok and cook at a sizzle for 5 minutes. Stir once to cook evenly. Transfer beans to plate and set aside.

3. In the same wok, heat 1 tablespoon oil over high flame. Add garlic and sizzle ½ minute.

4. Add ground beef and stir-fry 3 minutes, breaking up lumps.

5. Adjust flame to medium and, keeping beef mixture at a simmer, add beef sauce and cook, stirring 1 minute for sauce to simmer and thicken.

6. Add beans from plate and stir to mix. Serve.

7. To serve: Dish up on a round plate and serve hot. This dish can sit covered in a warm oven for 10 minutes.

8. Yield: Serves 2 alone or 6 in a 4-course dinner.

Notes: Other suitable vegetables to replace beans are broccoli slices, cucumber slices or spinach.

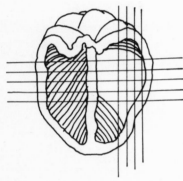

STIR-FRIED FLANK STEAK SLICES

IN BLACK BEAN SAUCE

INGREDIENTS:

2 cloves garlic, crushed and chopped
4 tablespoons fermented black beans, chopped coarsely
2 tablespoons peanut or vegetable oil
—
2 green peppers, cut into 1" pieces
—
Master sauce:
1 tablespoon dark soy
1 teaspoon cornstarch dissolved in ½ cup water
—
1 lb. flank steak, sliced ⅛" thick
2 tablespoons dark soy
1 teaspoon Chinese rice wine or sherry
½ teaspoon sugar
1 tablespoon cornstarch
—
2 tablespoons peanut or vegetable oil

TO PREPARE:

1. Chop garlic and black beans.
2. Remove seeds from green peppers and cut into 1" squares.
3. Make master sauce in a cup by combining dark soy and cornstarch solution.
4. Cut flank steak in half lengthwise; then cut crosswise into ⅛" slices. Mix together dark soy, wine, sugar, and cornstarch; mix well with meat and marinate ½ hour.

TO COOK: (cooking time about 15 minutes)

1. Heat 2 tablespoons oil in wok over medium flame. Add garlic and black beans, sizzle 1 minute.
2. Add green peppers, stir-fry 1 minute.
3. Add master sauce, cover wok, and simmer 5 minutes. Transfer sauce to a bowl and set aside.

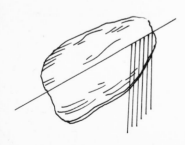

4. In the same wok, heat 2 tablespoons oil over high flame. Add beef and stir-fry quickly for 2 minutes. Mixture should be sizzling all the time.

5. Add the sauce from the bowl, stir-fry to mix for ½ minute. Serve.

6. To serve: Dish up in a plate and serve hot.

7. Yield: Serves 2 alone or 6 in a 4-course dinner.

**5 MINUTES
COOKING TIME**

STIR-FRIED FLANK STEAKS

IN OYSTER SAUCE

INGREDIENTS:

1 lb. flank steak, sliced ⅛" thick

—

Beef marinade:
1 tablespoon dark soy
1 tablespoon cornstarch
1 tablespoon Chinese rice wine or sherry
1 teaspoon sugar
½ teaspoon salt

—

4 tablespoons peanut or vegetable oil
6 thin slices fresh ginger
2 scallions, cut into 2" pieces
2 cloves garlic, crushed

—

Master sauce:
4 tablespoons oyster sauce
1 tablespoon dark soy
1 tablespoon sesame oil
½ teaspoon cornstarch

TO PREPARE:

1. Cut flank steak lengthwise into halves, trim fat. Cut each half crosswise into ⅛" slices. Make the beef marinade by combining all the ingredients, mix well with beef and marinate ½ hour.

2. Cut 6 thin slices ginger, and cut scallions into 2" pieces. Crush garlic.

3. Make master sauce by combining all the ingredients in a cup.

TO COOK: *(cooking time about 5 minutes)*

1. Heat 4 tablespoons oil in wok over high flame. Add ginger, scallions, and garlic. Sizzle 1 minute.

2. Add beef and stir-fry quickly at a sizzle for about 2 minutes, or to desired doneness. Flame must be high to seal in the juices.

3. Add master sauce and cook stirring ½ minute for sauce to simmer and thicken. Serve.

4. To serve: Dish up on a plate and serve at once, to savor the wok flavor.

5. Yield: Serves 2 alone or 6 in a 4-course dinner.

Notes: Stir-frying beef is the easiest and yet the hardest art to master in Chinese cooking. Be sure the actual cooking takes less than 5 minutes, and that meat is kept sizzling so the juices are sealed in the meat. There should be plenty of noise and stir-frying activity during the cooking.

ADDITIONAL RECIPE:

Stir-Fried Ground Beef and Chopped Smoked Oysters, see page 168

Chicken and Duck

INTRODUCTION

A lot of people hesitate to cook poultry Chinese style. They think that a whole bird is always used and that the bird must be chopped with a cleaver when it is prepared for cooking. This is not always true. There are many and varied methods of preparing a fowl. Most of the recipes here will deal with chicken breasts, wings, or other parts of the chicken. The Chinese are partial to chicken wings as many consider it the best part of the chicken. Another favorite is chicken feet, its soup with its rejuvenating quality makes it popular as a menu for women who have just given birth, or for people who feel weak or tired.

When a whole chicken or a whole duck is used, it is braised until the meat is ready to fall off the bones. There is no cutting or carving. You just bring the entire bird to the table and everyone tears a piece of meat off it with his chopsticks.

Think of the chicken parts that are available in the supermarkets in the United States—breasts, wings, halves, quarters. They are reasonably priced, high in protein and low in fat. In China it is very popular and is considered *ho bo sun* 好保身 (very healthy to the body). So, regretfully, it is always an expensive meat.

Chicken can be treated with all kinds of spices and seasonings, and it can usually sit in a warm oven without getting ruined while you prepare other dishes. These qualities make chicken a great dish for entertaining.

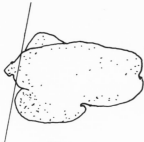

BRAISED SOY CHICKEN

WITH CHINESE MUSHROOMS

INGREDIENTS:

one 3—4 lb. whole chicken

—

Master sauce:
1 cup dark soy
1 tablespoon Chinese rice wine or sherry
2 cups water
1 tablespoon sugar
4 thin slices fresh ginger
½ teaspoon salt

—

12 Chinese mushrooms, soaked in water until soft

TO PREPARE:

1. Wash chicken and pat dry. Cut off and discard the small tail part.

2. Cut 4 thin slices fresh ginger.

3. Cut and discard stems of softened mushrooms.

4. Make master sauce by combining all the ingredients in a cup.

TO COOK: (cooking time about 1 hour)

1. In a heavy casserole large enough to hold the chicken, bring to boil the master sauce.

2. Add the chicken, breast down, cover pot and adjust flame to simmer gently ½ hour.

3. Turn the chicken over, add the mushrooms to the sauce, and simmer covered for ½ hour. Serve.

4. To serve: Chinese style, the chicken is served hot, and put whole on a platter with the mushrooms and sauce poured over it. Guests pick off the meat a morsel at a time with their chopsticks. The Chinese believe chicken tastes better if it is not cut with a knife, but you can, if you prefer, cut the chicken into serving pieces before bringing it to the table. This chicken can sit in its pot for hours, or overnight, and be reheated gently before serving. (In this case do not cut the chicken until it is reheated.)

5. Yield: Serves 4 alone or 6 in a 4-course dinner.

**25 MINUTES
COOKING TIME**

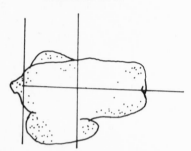

BRAISED LEMON CHICKEN

WITH SHALLOTS

INGREDIENTS:

one 2–3 lb. chicken, quartered
1 tablespoon dark soy
—
1 tablespoon peanut or vegetable oil
4 thin slices fresh ginger
20 shallots, peeled
—
Master sauce:
1 fresh lemon, juice and rind
1 tablespoon dark soy
1 tablespoon sugar
1 teaspoon sesame oil
½ teaspoon salt
1 cup water
—
1 teaspoon cornstarch dissolved in 1 tablespoon water

TO PREPARE:

1. Wash chicken and pat dry. Discard tail part. Quarter (or buy quartered chicken). Brush 1 tablespoon dark soy all over chicken skin.

2. Cut 4 thin slices fresh ginger.

3. Peel shallots.

4. Pare lemon rind into thin strips and chop. Reserve. Squeeze lemon juice and reserve.

5. Make master sauce in a cup by combining all the ingredients.

6. Make cornstarch solution. Set aside.

TO COOK: *(cooking time about 25 minutes)*

1. Use a casserole large enough to hold the chicken. It must have a tightly fitting lid. Heat 1 tablespoon oil in the casserole over medium flame. Add ginger and shallots and sizzle 1 minute.

2. Add chicken quarters. First brown skin side, and then the other side.

3. Add the master sauce; bring to a boil. Reduce flame, cover pot and simmer 15 minutes.

4. Lift out chicken, chop into bite-size pieces, arrange on a large platter and keep warm.

5. Bring the sauce and the shallots in the pot to a simmer, add cornstarch solution. Cook stirring ½ minute for sauce to simmer and thicken.

6. Pour sauce over chicken and serve at once.

7. To serve: Serve chicken pieces with sauce and shallots to each guest. Chicken can sit in its braising sauce for 1–2 hours as long as it is not carved. If dish is to be made ahead, reheat, then lift out chicken, carve, and thicken sauce. Serve immediately after carving.

8. Yield: Serves 4 alone or 6 in a 4-course dinner.

1 HOUR
COOKING TIME

BRAISED CHICKEN WINGS

IN OYSTER SAUCE

INGREDIENTS:

   2 lbs. chicken wings

   —

   2 scallions
   4 thin slices fresh ginger
   3 tablespoons peanut or vegetable oil

   —

   Master sauce:
   ½ cup oyster sauce
   1 tablespoon Chinese rice wine or sherry
   ¾ cup water
   1 tablespoon dark soy
   ½ teaspoon sugar
   1 teaspoon cornstarch
   ¼ teaspoon salt

TO PREPARE:

   1. Cut each chicken wing into 2 pieces by separating the wing section and the joint to which it is attached. Cut the wing section into three parts and the joint section into halves. Each wing will yield 5 pieces.

   2. Cut scallions into halves, and cut 4 thin slices of ginger.

   3. Make master sauce in a cup by combining all the ingredients.

TO COOK: *(cooking time about 1 hour)*

1. Heat 3 tablespoons oil in a heavy casserole over medium flame. Add scallions and ginger and sizzle ½ minute.

2. Add chicken wings and stir-fry 2 minutes.

3. Add the master sauce and bring to a boil. Cover pot, lower flame, and simmer 1 hour. Stir every 10 minutes to prevent sticking. Serve.

4. To serve: Serve hot in the casserole or place on a large platter. This dish can sit for hours or overnight; reheat to serve.

5. Yield: Serves 4 alone or 6 in a 4-course dinner.

20 MINUTES COOKING TIME

STEAMED CHICKEN BREASTS

WITH CHINESE MUSHROOMS

INGREDIENTS:

2 whole chicken breasts, cut into bite-size pieces

—

Master sauce:
1 teaspoon cornstarch dissolved in ½ cup water
1 tablespoon peanut or vegetable oil
3 tablespoons light soy
1 teaspoon Chinese rice wine or sherry
¼ teaspoon salt
½ teaspoon sugar

—

6 Chinese mushrooms soaked in water until soft, quartered

—

2 scallions, cut into 2″ pieces
4 thin slices fresh ginger

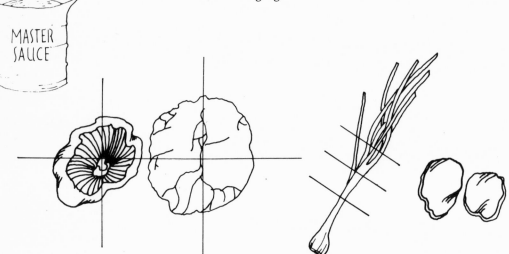

TO PREPARE:

1. Chop chicken breasts with heavy cleaver into 2″ x 1″ bite-size pieces.

2. Make the master sauce by combining all the ingredients and mix with chicken.

3. Discard stems and cut softened mushrooms in quarters.

4. Cut scallions into 2″ lengths, and cut 4 slices of ginger.

TO COOK: *(cooking time about 20 minutes)*

1. Prepare for steaming according to steaming instruction on page 2.

2. Place chicken and sauce on a heatproof pie plate; add mushrooms, scallions, and ginger; stir together to mix. This dish is now ready to steam.

3. Steam 20 minutes. Serve.

4. To serve: Serve hot either on steaming plate or transfer mixture onto a platter and serve.

5. Yield: Serves 2 alone or 6 in a 4-course dinner.

30 MINUTES
COOKING TIME

STEAMED CHICKEN BREASTS
SERVED IN OYSTER AND GINGER SAUCE

INGREDIENTS:

2 whole chicken breasts

—

3 tablespoons chicken broth collected from steaming
¼ teaspoon salt

—

Master sauce:
1 tablespoon peanut or vegetable oil
4 scallions, chopped fine
4 thin slices fresh ginger, chopped fine
½ cup oyster sauce
1 tablespoon dark soy
1 teaspoon cornstarch dissolved in ¼ cup water

TO PREPARE:

1. Wash chicken breast and pat dry.
2. Chop scallions and ginger.

TO COOK: *(cooking time about 30 minutes)*

1. Prepare for steaming according to steaming instructions on page 2. Place chicken breasts in a heatproof pie plate and steam 20 minutes.

2. Lift chicken out and cool. Reserve 3 tablespoons broth collected in the steaming plate.

3. Separate meat from bones with fingers. Discard bones and roughly cut up the meat into 1" chunks.

4. Mix together chicken meat, broth, and salt. Put in a serving plate, cover and keep warm in oven.

5. Make master sauce: Heat 1 tablespoon oil in a skillet over medium flame, add chopped scallions and ginger, and sizzle ½ minute. Add oyster sauce, dark soy and cornstarch solution. Cook stirring 1 minute for sauce to simmer and thicken.

6. To serve: Pour master sauce on top of chicken and serve immediately. The chicken meat can sit in a warm oven for ½ hour if the sauce is not added until directly before serving.

7. Yield: Serves 2 alone or 6 in a 4-course dinner.

**20 MINUTES
COOKING TIME**

COLD CHICKEN BREASTS

TRENT

INGREDIENTS:

2 whole chicken breasts
6 cups water

—

one 8-oz. can sliced bamboo shoots, drained
2 tablespoons white vinegar
1 teaspoon sugar
¼ teaspoon salt

—

Master sauce:
2—3 tablespoons red chili oil
4 tablespoons fish sauce (See page 15 for fish sauce.)
3 tablespoons white vinegar
2 tablespoons peanut or vegetable oil
2 tablespoons sesame oil
½ teaspoon salt
black pepper

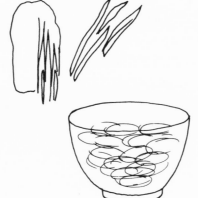

TO PREPARE:

1. Drain sliced bamboo shoots and marinate in vinegar, sugar, and salt for ½ hour.

2. Make master sauce by combining all the ingredients in a cup. Set aside. Vary amounts of chili oil and vinegar to taste.

TO COOK: *(cooking time about 20 minutes)*

1. Bring to boil 6 cups of water in a large pot. Add chicken breasts, cover pot, and simmer 20 minutes. Lift out and cool.

2. Separate meat from chicken and discard the bones. Shred meat with fingers to thin 2" x ¼" strips. Put in a large bowl and chill.

3. To serve: In a large bowl, toss together the shredded chicken meat, the bamboo slices, and the master sauce. Chill till ready to serve. Arrange mixture on a platter and serve cold. This dish can be covered with plastic wrap and sit in the refrigerator for hours or overnight.

4. Yield: Serves 2 alone or 6 in a 4-course dinner.

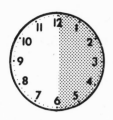

30 MINUTES
COOKING TIME

BOILED CHICKEN SERVED COLD

IN SPICY SESAME SAUCE

INGREDIENTS:

1 whole chicken, quartered
6 cups water
—
3 scallions, white part only
2 stalks celery, cut into thin strips
—
Sesame sauce:
3 tablespoons sesame oil
2 tablespoons peanut or vegetable oil
1 tablespoon hot brown bean sauce
2 tablespoons light soy
1 teaspoon sugar
salt to taste

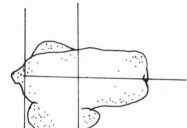

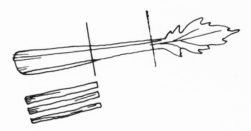

TO PREPARE:

1. Wash chicken quarters, pat dry. Cut and discard tail part.

2. Cut scallions into 2" pieces, then into 2" x ⅛" strips.

3. Wash and peel celery stalks, cut into 2" pieces, then into 2" x ⅛" strips.

4. Make sesame sauce by combining all the ingredients in a bowl. Set aside.

TO COOK: *(cooking time about 30 minutes)*

1. Bring to boil 6 cups of water in a pot. Add chicken and cover. Simmer 20 minutes. Lift out and cool.

2. Separate chicken meat with fingers, discard skin and bone. Shred meat into 3" x ½" pieces.

3. Put meat in a large bowl; add scallions and celery. Mix, cover bowl, and chill.

4. To serve: Pour sesame sauce into chicken bowl, toss to mix well, and serve cold or at room temperature. The chicken, scallions, and celery can be prepared well in advance, and so can the sauce. Toss to mix when ready to serve.

5. Yield: Serves 4 alone or 6 in a 4-course dinner.

6 MINUTES
COOKING TIME

STIR-FRIED DICED CHICKEN BREASTS

IN HOISIN SAUCE

INGREDIENTS:

4 chicken breasts; boned, skinned, and diced
4 tablespoons peanut or vegetable oil
—

1 medium green pepper, seeds removed and diced
one 8-oz. can sliced bamboo shoots, drained and diced
—

Master sauce:
4 tablespoons hoisin sauce
1 tablespoon dark soy
½ teaspoon salt
1 tablespoon corn starch dissolved in 1 tablespoon water

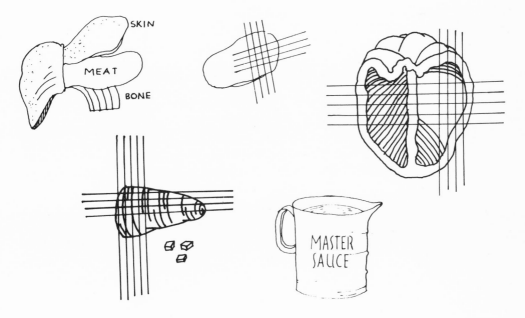

TO PREPARE:

1. If necessary, bone and skin chicken breast. Cut meat into ¼″ dice.

2. Remove seeds and cut green pepper into ¼″ dice.

3. Drain and cut sliced bamboo shoots into ¼″ dice.

4. Make master sauce by combining all ingredients in a cup.

TO COOK: *(cooking time about 6 minutes)*

1. Heat 4 tablespoons oil in wok over high flame. Add chicken dices and stir-fry 3 minutes.

2. Add diced green pepper and bamboo shoots. Stir-fry 2 minutes.

3. Add master sauce and cook stirring 1 minute for sauce to simmer and thicken. Serve.

4. To serve: Dish up on a plate and serve hot at once for its wok flavor.

5. Yield: Serves 2 alone or 6 in a 4-course dinner.

Notes: You may add 1 tablespoon hot brown bean sauce or ½ teaspoon chili sauce to give this dish a hot Szechuan taste.

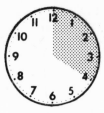

STIR-FRIED CHICKEN BREASTS

IN GARLIC AND BLACK BEAN SAUCE

20 MINUTES
COOKING TIME

INGREDIENTS:

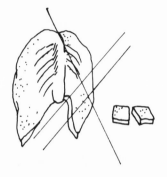

2 whole chicken breasts, cut into 1" x 2" pieces

—

8 cloves garlic, crushed and chopped fine
4 tablespoons fermented black beans, chopped coarsely
3 tablespoons peanut or vegetable oil

—

Master sauce:
1 tablespoon dark soy
½ teaspoon salt
½ teaspoon sugar
1 teaspoon Chinese rice wine or sherry

TO PREPARE:

    1. Chop chicken breasts into 1" x 2" pieces.

    2. Chop garlic and black beans.

    3. Make master sauce by combining all the ingredients in a cup.

TO COOK: *(cooking time about 20 minutes)*

    1. Heat 3 tablespoons oil in wok over high flame. Add garlic and black beans and sizzle 2 minutes.

    2. Add chicken and stir-fry, sizzling 5 minutes.

    3. Lower flame, cover wok, and simmer 5 minutes.

    4. Add master sauce, and cook stirring 2 minutes for sauce to simmer and thicken. Be sure to keep turning the chicken so it's coated with sauce. Serve.

    5. To serve: Dish up on a large plate and serve at once to preserve the fresh garlicky taste.

    6. Yield: Serves 2 alone or 6 in a 4-course dinner.

DEEP-FRIED PAPER-WRAPPED

CHICKEN PIECES IN FIVE-SPICES

INGREDIENTS:

1 whole frying chicken, quartered

—

Master sauce:
2 tablespoons dark soy
2 tablespoons light soy
1 teaspoon sugar
1 teaspoon Chinese rice wine or sherry
1 teaspoon five-spices powder

—

wax paper, cut into 6" squares

—

4 cups peanut or vegetable oil

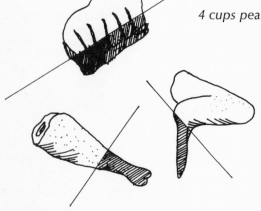

TO PREPARE:

1. Chop away all bony parts of chicken like the back, rib cages, tips of the wings and the drumsticks. Chop the chicken into bite-size pieces (about 16).

2. Make the master sauce by combining all the ingredients in a cup. Add to chicken, mix well and marinate 1 hour.

3. Cut 16 pieces wax paper 6" square to wrap the chicken.

4. Shake each piece of chicken free of excess marinade, wrap in wax paper envelope fashion. Be sure ends are tucked in securely.

TO COOK: *(cooking time about 30 minutes)*

1. Heat 4 cups oil in wok over medium flame. Add half of the wrapped chicken pieces, and deep fry 15 minutes to golden brown. Keep turning the pieces to fry evenly. Lift out and drain, keep warm in the oven.

2. Fry the rest. Serve.

3. To serve: Arrange wrapped chicken pieces on a platter and serve hot. Guests will themselves unwrap the chicken and discard paper. This dish can sit in a warm oven for ½ hour.

4. Yield: Serves 4 alone or 6 in a 4-course dinner.

Notes: An alternate method of cooking the chicken pieces is to wrap them in 6″ aluminum foil envelopes, and put them on baking sheet in a very hot oven (about 450° F). Bake 45 minutes—1 hour.

2 HOURS
COOKING TIME

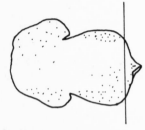

BRAISED APRICOT-FLAVORED DUCK

IN HOISIN SAUCE

INGREDIENTS:

one 4 lb. duck

—

Master sauce:
4 scallions
¼ cup apricot jam
½ cup hoisin sauce
4 tablespoons dark soy
½ teaspoon salt
3 cups water

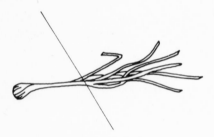

TO PREPARE:

    1. Wash duck and pat dry. Cut and discard tail part.

    2. Cut scallions into halves.

    3. Make master sauce by combining all ingredients in a cup.

TO COOK: *(cooking time about 2 hours)*

    1. Use a large heavy casserole with a fitting lid. The duck should fit snugly at the bottom of the casserole. Place the casserole over a low flame, add the duck, and brown lightly on all sides slowly for 20 minutes. The thick fat will run out; drain this fat off.

2. In a saucepan bring to boil the master sauce. Pour sauce over the duck, cover casserole, lower flame, and simmer 1½ hours.

3. Turn duck every 15 minutes to prevent sticking. The *hoisin* and apricot sauce get burned easily, so be sure the flame is very low and the duck is turned often.

4. After 1½ hours simmering, remove duck to a large platter and keep warm.

5. Skim off all the fat from the sauce with a baster or ladle. Boil rapidly to reduce the sauce to 2 cups.

6. To serve: Use 2 spoons to slightly separate meat and joints from duck carcass, pour the sauce over, and serve hot. Eat Chinese-style by picking meat off duck with chopsticks one morsel at a time. The duck can sit for hours or overnight; reheat to serve.

7. Yield: Serves 4 alone or 6 in a 4-course dinner.

Notes: For a more substantial meal, line the platter with a bed of cooked spinach, then top with duck and sauce. If you have a Chinese plum sauce, or a duck sauce, you can use it instead of apricot jam.

2 HOURS
COOKING TIME

BRAISED ONION DUCK

IN DARK SOY

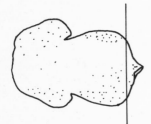

INGREDIENTS:

one 3—4 lb. duck

—

1 lb. onions, thinly sliced

—

Master sauce:
2 cups water
½ cup dark soy
1 tablespoon Chinese rice wine or sherry
2 thin slices fresh ginger
1 teaspoon sugar
2 star anise
salt to taste

—

1 tablespoon cornstarch dissolved in 1 tablespoon water

TO PREPARE:

1. Wash the duck and pat dry. Cut and discard tail part.
2. Slice onions about ⅛" thick.
3. Cut 2 thin slices fresh ginger.
4. Make master sauce in a cup by combining all the ingredients.
5. Dissolve cornstarch in water. Reserve.

TO COOK: *(cooking time about 2 hours)*

1. Use a heavy casserole large enough to hold the duck. Set casserole over low flame, add the duck, and brown lightly on all sides for the fat to run out. Lift out duck, pour away all but 1 tablespoon of the fat.

MASTER SAUCE

2. Set casserole back on a medium flame, add onions, and stir-fry 2 minutes.
3. Add master sauce and bring to a boil.
4. Return the duck to the casserole, lower the flame, cover the pot and simmer about 1¾ hours. Turn duck every ½ hour to prevent sticking.

5. Lift out duck, place in a deep platter and keep warm in the oven.

6. Bring the sauce in the pot to a boil, add cornstarch solution, cook stirring 1 minute for the sauce to simmer and thicken.

7. To serve: Pour sauce over duck and serve hot. This dish can sit in a warm oven for hours or overnight in a refrigerator; reheat to serve. Serve the duck Chinese-style—guests pick meat off duck with chopsticks one morsel at a time.

8. Yield: Serves 4 alone or 6 in a 4-course dinner.

Vegetables

INTRODUCTION

Welcome to the "crunchy" world of Chinese vegetables. Anyone who has eaten Chinese food will say, "Oh, those delicious, healthy, crunchy vegetables." But, did you know that many Chinese vegetables are cooked and served non-crunchy?

Chinese celery cabbage, for example, is the ideal vegetable for braising; steeped in flavor, it will glide down your throat softly. Or take braised lettuce, or *bok choy* with mushroom, or braised cucumber, or eggplant. . . .

But there are many crunchy, crispy vegetables—green broccoli, snow peas, *bok choy*, beansprouts, spinach, and bamboo shoots! These are the important steps to follow if you want to prepare crunchy vegetables:

1. Large pieces of vegetable should be slant-cut (see Chapter 2 on Cutting). This provides pointed, angular pieces with more cooking surface than thick, blunt-ended, straight-cut pieces. The slant-cut allows the pieces to cook uniformly in a short time, and they have more surface per piece to absorb seasoning and sauces.

2. Use a hot wok with sizzling oil so that the vegetable juice is sealed in the minute it touches the wok.

3. Do not add anything to the vegetables—either seasonings or sauce or meat—until the vegetables are cooked to desired crunchiness and are just about to be dished up. (Salt is the exception to this rule; it is added to keep the vegetables green and crisp.) This means that in a combined meat and vegetable dish, the two ingredients must be cooked separately. The meat is cooked first and set aside; then the vegetables are cooked quickly and the two ingredients combined with a quick toss only at the last minute.

40 MINUTES
COOKING TIME

BRAISED WHOLE CUCUMBERS

WITH CHINESE MUSHROOMS

INGREDIENTS:

*4 medium size whole cucumbers, peeled, halved, and
with seeds removed*

—

3 tablespoons peanut or vegetable oil
2 thin slices fresh ginger

—

1 cup water
6 Chinese mushrooms soaked in water until soft
3 tablespoons light soy
1 teaspoon salt

TO PREPARE:

1. Peel cucumbers, halve, and remove seeds.
2. Cut 2 thin slices ginger.
3. Discard stems and cut softened mushrooms into ¼"
strips.

TO COOK: *(cooking time about 40 minutes)*

1. Heat 3 tablespoons oil over medium flame in a casserole large enough to hold the cucumber flat. Add ginger and
sizzle ½ minute.

2. Add cucumbers and sizzle a few seconds on one side.

3. Add water, mushrooms, light soy, and salt. Bring to
a boil quickly. Cover pot, lower flame, and simmer 30 minutes. Serve.

4. To serve: Place cucumbers carefully on a large platter
without breaking them. Pour over mushrooms and sauce and
serve very hot. This dish can sit in the pot for hours, be reheated to serve.

5. Yield: Serves 6 in a 4-course dinner.

15 MINUTES
COOKING TIME

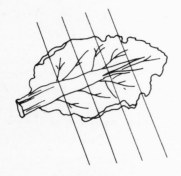

BRAISED CHINESE CELERY CABBAGE

WITH DRIED SHRIMPS

INGREDIENTS:

10 dried shrimps, soaked until soft in 1 cup water
2 thin slices fresh ginger
3 tablespoons peanut or vegetable oil

—

1 whole Chinese celery cabbage, cut into ½" pieces

—

4 ozs. cellophane noodles, covered in water and soaked until soft
1 teaspoon salt

TO PREPARE:

1. Soak shrimps until soft in 1 cup water.

2. Cut 2 thin slices fresh ginger.

3. Separate and wash stalks of celery cabbage. Cut stalks crosswise into ½" lengths.

4. Cover cellophane noodles and soak till soft. Drain.

TO COOK: *(cooking time about 15 minutes)*

1. Heat 3 tablespoons oil in wok over medium heat. Add ginger and dry shrimps (reserve shrimp liquid for later use). Stir-fry 1 minute.

2. Add celery cabbage and stir-fry 2 minutes.

3. Add shrimp liquid and bring to a simmer.

4. Add cellophane noodles and salt. Cover wok, lower flame and simmer 10 minutes. Serve.

5. To serve: Dish up on a plate and serve hot. This dish can sit in a warm oven for about 10 minutes. Or cook early and reheat to serve.

6. Yield: Serves 6 in a 4-course dinner.

20 MINUTES
COOKING TIME

BRAISED EGGPLANTS

WITH DRIED SHRIMPS

INGREDIENTS:

2 medium eggplants cut into strips
4 cloves garlic, crushed
4 tablespoons peanut or vegetable oil

—

10 dried shrimps, soaked in ½ cup water until soft

—

Master sauce:
2 tablespoons light soy
1 teaspoon sugar
½ teaspoon salt
1 tablespoon sesame oil

TO PREPARE:

1. Cut eggplants (do not peel) crosswise into 4″ thick slices. Then cut into ¼″ strips.
2. Crush garlic.
3. Soak dry shrimps until soft in ½ cup water. Crush coarsely in same water. Reserve.
4. Make master sauce by combining all the ingredients in a cup.

TO COOK: *(cooking time about 20 minutes)*

1. Heat 4 tablespoons oil in wok over medium flame. Add garlic and sizzle ½ minute. Add eggplants and stir-fry 3 minutes.
2. Add crushed dried shrimps in their ½ cup of water and the master sauce. Bring quickly to a boil.
3. Cover wok, lower flame, and simmer for 10 minutes. Serve.
4. To serve: Dish up on a platter and serve hot, warm, or cold. This dish can keep in the refrigerator for a couple of days and is good served cold.
5. Yield: Serves 6 in a 4-course dinner.

10 MINUTES
COOKING TIME

QUICK BOILED LETTUCE

SERVED WITH OYSTER SAUCE

INGREDIENTS:

2 heads fresh lettuce (preferably iceberg)

—

8 cups water
2 tablespoons peanut or vegetable oil
2 teaspoons salt

—

1 tablespoon peanut or vegetable oil
½ cup oyster sauce

TO PREPARE:

Separate leaves of lettuce under running water. Wash and drain.

TO COOK: *(cooking time about 10 minutes)*

1. Bring to boil in a large pot the water, oil, and salt.
2. Keeping water at a rapid boil, add half of the lettuce. Boil 1 minute. Keep turning the leaves to cook them evenly.
3. Drain lettuce in strainer, put on a large platter, and keep warm.
4. Working very quickly, put the rest of the lettuce to boil. Drain it and pile on the platter.
5. To serve: Dribble oil and oyster sauce on the lettuce and serve hot at once to taste the crunchiness of the lettuce. Overboiling will wilt the leaves and turn them yellow. Work quickly so that lettuce is piping hot.
6. Yield: Serves 6 in a 4-course dinner.

Notes: This is a common method of serving vegetables in China, for it retains all the freshness of crisp vegetables; and is very simple to prepare. Other vegetables suitable for this dish are watercress, spinach, and broccoli.

**6 MINUTES
COOKING TIME**

STIR-FRIED SPINACH

WITH GROUND BEEF

INGREDIENTS:

1 lb. fresh spinach, cut into 2" pieces
2 tablespoons peanut or vegetable oil
2 cloves garlic, crushed
¼ teaspoon salt

—

½ lb. ground beef
2 tablespoons peanut or unflavored vegetable oil
1 clove garlic, crushed

—

Master sauce:
2 tablespoons dark soy
1 teaspoon Chinese rice wine or sherry
1 teaspoon sugar
2 teaspoons cornstarch dissolved in ¼ cup water
¼ teaspoon salt
white pepper

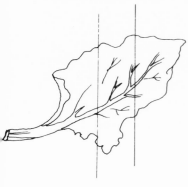

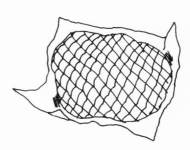

TO PREPARE:

1. Wash spinach and cut into 2" pieces.
2. Crush garlic.
3. Make master sauce in a cup by combining all the ingredients.

119

TO COOK: *(cooking time about 6 minutes)*

1. Heat 2 tablespoons oil in wok over medium flame. Add garlic and sizzle ½ minute.

2. Add spinach and salt and stir-fry 2 minutes. Transfer to plate and keep warm.

3. Heat 2 tablespoons oil in the same wok over high flame. Add garlic and sizzle ½ minute.

4. Add ground beef and stir-fry 2 minutes, breaking any lumps.

5. Add master sauce and cook stirring 1 minute for sauce to simmer and thicken. Pour beef over spinach and serve.

6. To serve: Be sure to serve the spinach hot and that the beef and its sauce are piled attractively on top.

7. Yield: Serves 2 alone or 6 in a 4-course dinner.

**6 MINUTES
COOKING TIME**

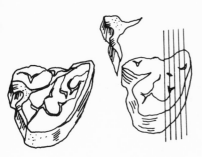

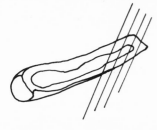

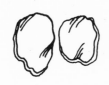

STIR-FRIED CUCUMBER SLICES

WITH PORK

INGREDIENTS:

2 thin pork chops, cut into ⅛″ slices

—

Pork marinade:
1 tablespoon light soy
1 teaspoon cornstarch
½ teaspoon Chinese rice wine or sherry
½ teaspoon sugar
¼ teaspoon salt

3 cucumbers, peeled, halved, and with seeds removed
2 tablespoons peanut or vegetable oil
2 thin slices fresh ginger
¼ teaspoon salt

—

2 tablespoons peanut or vegetable oil

TO PREPARE:

1. Discard bone and trim excess fat off pork chops. Lay chops flat on board and cut into slices ⅛″ thick.
2. Make pork marinade and mix well with pork slices; marinate ½ hour.
3. Peel cucumbers, halve, and remove seeds. Slice ⅙″ thick.
4. Cut 2 thin slices fresh ginger.

TO COOK: *(cooking time about 6 minutes)*

1. Heat 2 tablespoons oil in wok over medium flame. Add ginger and sizzle ½ minute.
2. Add cucumber slices and salt. Stir-fry 2—3 minutes. Transfer to plate and keep warm.
3. Heat 2 tablespoons oil in the same wok over high flame. Add marinated pork slices and stir-fry briskly 3 minutes.
4. Add the cooked cucumber to the pork. Stir to mix. Serve.
5. To serve: Dish up on a plate and serve hot at once. Do not let dish sit because the cucumber will ooze liquid.
6. Yield: Serves 2 alone or 6 in a 4-course dinner.

STIR-FRIED SNOW PEAS

WITH CELERY AND SCALLIONS

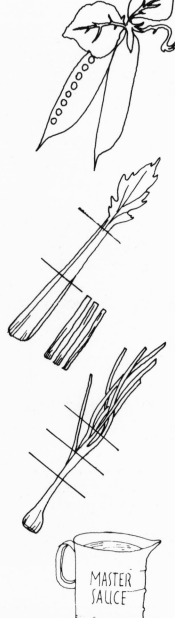

**5 MINUTES
COOKING TIME**

INGREDIENTS:

½ lb. snow pea pods, strings removed
3 stalks celery, cut into 2" x ¼" strips
4 scallions, cut into 2" pieces
3 tablespoons peanut or vegetable oil
½ teaspoon salt
½ teaspoon sugar
—
Master sauce:
1 teaspoon cornstarch dissolved in ¼ cup water
2 tablespoons light soy

TO PREPARE:

1. Wash and remove strings from snow pea pods.
2. Remove strings from celery stalks, cut into 2" pieces, then into 2" x ¼" strips.
3. Cut scallions into 2" pieces.
4. Make master sauce by combining cornstarch and light soy.

TO COOK: (cooking time about 5 minutes)

1. Heat 3 tablespoons oil in wok over high flame. Add snow peas, celery, scallions, salt and sugar. Stir-fry at a sizzle for 3 minutes.
2. Add master sauce and stir-fry 1 minute for sauce to simmer and thicken. Serve.
3. To serve: Dish up on a plate and serve at once hot. This dish cannot be reheated as the vegetables will go limp.
4. Yield: Serves 6 in a 4-course dinner.

ADDITIONAL RECIPES:

Stir-Fried Monk-Style Vegetarian Dish, see page 152
Stir-Fried Fresh Broccoli in Light Soy, see page 154
Braised Chinese Mushrooms and Bok Choy in Dark Soy, see page 156
Cucumber and Celery Salad, see page 157
Stir-Fried Beansprouts with Roast Pork, see page 171

Beancurd and Eggs

INTRODUCTION

Two of the less expensive but very nourishing foods are beancurds and eggs. Perhaps that's why millions of people in China are healthy on this high protein diet.

Beancurd is made by boiling freshly ground soybeans into a milky soup. A curdling agent, gypsum, is added, and the beancurd is then poured into large trays where it sets into a custard-like substance which can be cut into 2″ by 2″ cubes. These cubes are sold fresh in Chinese or Japanese stores. The milky cubes have a creamy, smooth texture, and when braised quickly in oyster sauce or a hot Szechuan sauce, they are my husband Peter's favorite dish.

Whenever I ask him, "*Wong Duck* [his Chinese name given by my family; Duck means virtue and is also phonetically linked to Trent] *joan-yee sic mud yeah?*" ("like eat what thing?") He'll answer promptly, "*Sic dull-fu.*" ("Eat beancurd.")

If we're among Chinese friends, this reply will draw a lot of giggles and teasing. For "*sic dull-fu*" also means a dirty old man pinching a younger girl. Why? Because there's nothing quite so soft, smooth, and tantalizing as eating *dull-fu!*

A similar texture to *dull-fu* is that of steamed, beaten eggs. So, if you haven't yet tasted beancurd or cannot get it easily, rush into the kitchen now and make some steamed eggs.

Every child in a Chinese family literally grows up on steamed eggs, mixed with plain rice. It is almost like strained baby food; nutritious, tasty, and with no worries for the mother about bones or large chunks of solids. It is also economical, since eggs are inexpensive in China and the dish is steamed over rice so no extra fuel for cooking is needed.

Egg dishes often form part of the Chinese main course and are not breakfast or snack items. They are economical and easy to make, so do include them if you're planning a multi-course dinner and are looking for variety.

20 MINUTES
COOKING TIME

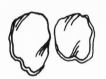

BRAISED HARD BOILED EGGS

WITH CHICKEN LIVERS

INGREDIENTS:

4 eggs

—

½ cup dark soy
1 cup water
1 teaspoon sugar
2 thin slices fresh ginger
dash of salt

—

½ lb. chicken livers

TO PREPARE:

1. Hard boil 4 eggs, and remove shells.
2. Cut 2 thin slices fresh ginger.
3. Cut the chicken livers in halves.

TO COOK: *(cooking time about 20 minutes)*

1. In a heavy pot bring the dark soy, water, sugar, ginger, and salt to a boil.

2. Add chicken livers and bring to the boil again uncovered.

3. Add eggs and cover pot, lower flame, and simmer 15 minutes. Serve.

4. To serve: Quarter the eggs and put on a large plate, arrange livers on top, and pour the sauce over. Serve hot. This dish can sit in the pot for hours or overnight. When ready to serve, reheat, cut eggs, and serve.

5. Yield: Serves 2 alone or 6 in a 4-course dinner.

Notes: This makes a good cocktail tidbit, served hot or cold, or bubbling in a fondue pot.

8 MINUTES
COOKING TIME

STEAMED EGG CUSTARD

WITH LIGHT SOY

INGREDIENTS:

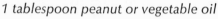

4 eggs, beaten thoroughly

—

water (1½ volume of eggs, that is, each egg needs 3 half
    eggshells of water)
½ teaspoon salt

—

1 tablespoon peanut or vegetable oil
1 tablespoon light soy
2 scallions cut into ⅛" rings

TO PREPARE:

1. Beat 4 eggs well but avoid allowing them to foam.
2. Add 12 half-eggshells of water and salt to taste; beat
to mix.
3. Pour eggs into a 2–3" deep heatproof pie plate or
platter. The dish is now ready to steam.
4. Cut scallions into ⅛" rings.

TO COOK: (cooking time about 8 minutes)

1. Prepare for steaming according to steaming instructions on page 2.
2. Using a very gentle steam, put egg mixture to steam
for 8 minutes or until egg is set. Opening lid during steaming
won't ruin the dish. Do not overcook or use a strong steam,
as this will toughen the eggs and they will have holes on the
surface instead of being smooth.
3. To serve: Pour oil and light soy on the eggs and garnish with scallion rings. Serve hot at once. Put eggs to steam
when it is 8 minutes before dinner time so that the dish is
ready to serve at once.
4. Yield: Serves 6 in a 4-course dinner.

STEAMED EGG CUSTARD WITH DRIED SHRIMPS

AND CELLOPHANE NOODLES

INGREDIENTS:

4 eggs, well beaten

—

water (12 half-eggshells of water)
½ teaspoon salt

—

16 dried shrimps, soaked in water until soft
2 ozs. cellophane noodles, soaked in water until soft

—

1 tablespoon peanut or vegetable oil
1 tablespoon light soy

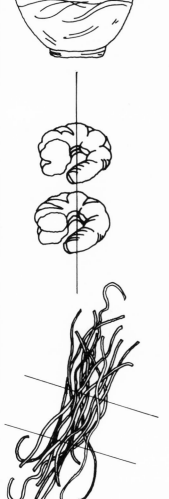

TO PREPARE:

1. Beat eggs well but avoid foaming. Add water and salt and beat well to mix.

2. Cut softened dried shrimps into halves.

3. Cut softened cellophane noodles into 1″ lengths.

TO COOK: *(cooking time about 8 minutes)*

1. Prepare for steaming according to steaming instructions on page 2.

2. Pour egg mixture into a 2–3″ deep heatproof pie plate. Add soaked shrimps and cellophane noodles. Steam 8 minutes in a gentle steam. Serve.

3. To serve: Add oil and light soy on top of custard and serve hot at once in its steaming plate. Steam eggs for 8 minutes before you're ready to serve dinner as this dish cannot sit or be overcooked.

4. Yield: Serves 2 alone or 6 in a 4-course dinner.

5 MINUTES
COOKING TIME

STIR-FRIED EGGS WITH CRABMEAT

AND SCALLIONS

INGREDIENTS:

4 scallions, cut into 2" x ⅛" strips
2 tablespoons peanut or vegetable oil
—

one 6-oz. package frozen crabmeat, drained and
  coarsely shredded
—

4 eggs, beaten thoroughly
1 tablespoon light soy
1 teaspoon sesame oil
dash of salt and white pepper

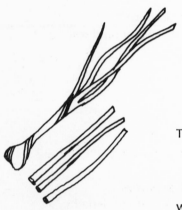

TO PREPARE:

1. Cut scallions into 2" lengths, then into 2" x ⅛" strips.
2. Defrost crabmeat, drain, and shred meat coarsely.
3. Beat 4 eggs well. Add light soy, sesame oil, salt, and white pepper. Beat to mix.

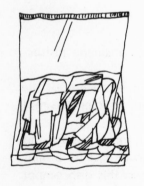

TO COOK: *(cooking time about 5 minutes)*

1. Heat 2 tablespoons oil in wok over medium flame, add scallions, and sizzle ½ minute.
2. Add crabmeat to egg mixture, stir to mix, pour mixture into wok and stir-fry till eggs are soft but not runny, about 2 minutes. Use an under-and-over stir-fry sweep to scramble the eggs.
3. To serve: Dish up in a plate and serve hot.
4. Yield: Serves 2 alone or 6 in a 4-course dinner.

20 MINUTES
COOKING TIME

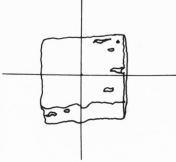

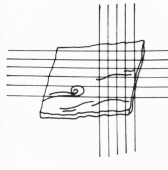

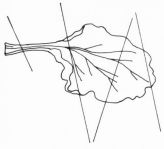

BRAISED BEANCURD WITH BOK CHOY

IN FISH SAUCE

INGREDIENTS:

6 pieces fresh beancurd
2 tablespoons peanut or vegetable oil
2 thin slices fresh ginger

—

4 thin slices cooked ham, cut into 1″ squares
1 teaspoon Chinese rice wine or sherry
3 tablespoons fish sauce (see page 15)
½ cup water

—

2 small bok choy, slant-cut into 2″ pieces
½ teaspoon salt

TO PREPARE:

1. Quarter beancurds.
2. Cut 2 thin slices fresh ginger.
3. Cut ham into 1″ squares.
4. Separate bok choy stalks, wash, and drain. Slant-cut into 2″ pieces.

TO COOK: (cooking time about 20 minutes)

1. Heat 2 tablespoons oil in a heavy casserole over medium flame. Add ginger and sizzle ½ minute.
2. Add beancurds and sizzle ½ minute.
3. Add ham, wine, fish sauce, and water. Bring to a boil uncovered.
4. Add bok choy and salt, bring to a boil, lower flame, cover pot, and simmer 15 minutes. Serve.
5. To serve: Serve hot in the casserole. The broth in this dish can be spooned over rice as a sauce. This dish can sit in the covered pot for 1 hour or so. Reheat gently to serve so as not to overcook the bok choy or beancurd.
6. Yield: Serves 2 alone or 6 in a 4-course dinner.

Notes: Substitute lettuce for bok choy if necessary. Light soy can be used instead of fish sauce if fish sauce is not available.

STIR-FRIED BEANCURD

IN OYSTER SAUCE

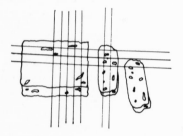

INGREDIENTS:

    6 pieces fresh beancurd, cut into ½" squares
    3 tablespoons peanut or vegetable oil
    2 thin slices fresh ginger

    —

    1 8-oz. package frozen green peas

    —

    Master sauce:
    ¼ cup oyster sauce
    2 tablespoons dark soy
    ½ teaspoon sugar
    1 tablespoon cornstarch dissolved in ¼ cup water
    1 teaspoon sesame oil
    ¼ teaspoon salt

TO PREPARE:

    1. Cut beancurd into ½" squares.

    2. Cut 2 thin slices fresh ginger.

    3. Cook peas in water according to directions on package. Drain and reserve.

    4. Make master sauce by combining all the ingredients in a cup.

TO COOK: *(cooking time about 5 minutes)*

    1. Heat 3 tablespoons oil in wok over medium flame. Add ginger and sizzle ½ minute.

    2. Add beancurd and stir-fry gently 2 minutes. Take care not to mash beancurd.

    3. Add green peas and stir-fry ½ minute to mix.

    4. Keep mixture at a simmer, add master sauce and cook stirring 2 minutes for sauce to simmer and thicken. Serve.

    5. To serve: Dish up in a large bowl and serve hot at once. This dish can sit in a warm oven for 5 minutes.

    6. Yield: Serves 2 alone or 6 in a 4-course dinner.

MASTER
SAUCE

5 MINUTES
COOKING TIME

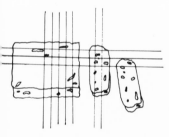

STIR-FRIED BEANCURD

IN HOT BROWN BEAN SAUCE

INGREDIENTS:

½ lb. roast pork, chopped coarsely
2 thin slices fresh ginger
2 tablespoons peanut or vegetable oil

6 pieces fresh beancurd, cut into 1" squares

Hot sauce:
1—2 tablespoons hot brown bean sauce
1 tablespoon dark soy
2 teaspoons cornstarch dissolved in ½ cup water
1 teaspoon sesame oil
½ teaspoon sugar
dash salt

TO PREPARE:

1. Chop roast pork coarsely.
2. Cut 2 thin slices fresh ginger.
3. Cut beancurd into 1" squares.
4. Make hot sauce by combining all the ingredients in a cup.

TO COOK: *(cooking time about 5 minutes)*

1. Heat 2 tablespoons oil in wok over medium flame. Add ginger and roast pork, stir-fry 1 minute.
2. Add beancurd, and stir-fry 1 minute. Do not mash up beancurd.
3. Keep mixture at a simmer, add hot sauce, and cook stirring 1 minute for sauce to simmer and thicken. Serve.
4. To serve: Dish up in a large bowl and serve hot at once.
5. Yield: Serves 2 alone or 6 in a 4-course dinner.

Notes: If roast pork is not available, substitute diced cooked ham.

Rice and Noodles

RICE

Rice and noodles form the starchy bulk of a Chinese meal, comparable to the bread, potatoes, or the spaghetti of a Western diet.

The Chinese have a great respect for rice, knowing the back-breaking labor that goes into its growing and harvesting in China. To leave even a grain of rice in the rice bowl is considered the height of waste and bad manners. A child is taught that he'll have a pockmark on his face for every grain left in his rice bowl.

Many people who do not understand how the Chinese eat their food, pile the food and sauce into their rice bowl until the rice becomes soggy and unsightly. No wonder half the bowl of rice with its soggy sauce is left uneaten! Remember that in eating Chinese food, a rice bowl should not be treated like a plate; there should be nothing in it but the rice and the morsel of food you are eating at the moment.

Notice how the Chinese eat in a restaurant. You will see that there is much reaching out for little morsels of food which are eaten at once, or which rest briefly in the bowl. The rice itself remains relatively free of sauce, and in that way, the individual taste of each dish is better savored. We do pour sauces on our rice, but only a little at a time and that patch of rice is then eaten immediately. We would never pour on a lot of sauce, stir up the rice with our chopsticks, and then pile more food on top of that!

Plain boiled white rice is always served in a multi-course Chinese dinner so that you can taste the various dishes more clearly. Fried rice should be a separate dish; it is either to be eaten alone as a quick snack, or when it is included in an elaborate banquet, it's served last after all the other plates of food have been cleared away.

Fried rice is usually made from left-over rice; this is how we use it up. The rice is both less sticky and harder after sitting overnight, and the logical way to reuse it is to fry it in oil. Personally, I like fried rice only if it's made from freshly cooked rice so that it's hot and fluffy.

On the whole, the Chinese do not like converted rice (which is unheard of in China). They prefer either the oval raw white rice which, when cooked, is soft and moist, or the long-grain raw white rice. The glutinous, sticky rice is used mainly for sweets in Chinese cooking, unlike the Japanese who use it for many meals.

NOODLES

Noodles are basically a snack served at odd hours of the day. In North China, it forms part of the staple diet when rice is scarce. Noodles make an ideal light lunch or late supper. Noodles are seldom served at a dinner except with the fried rice at the end of an elaborate banquet where no plain rice has been served, for those who are still hungry.

Noodles can be a little meal in themselves, as they are always seasoned with pieces of meat and vegetables, whether they're served fried or in soup form. It is a common practice to share a plate of noodles in a restaurant when you're ordering a snack, especially in a *dim sum* parlor. There, your main concern, of course, is for the tiny pieces of dumplings, and the noodle dish is something to fill up the very hungry.

Cooking noodles is like cooking spaghetti—the first step is to boil them until they are soft. They are then drained and either fried or added to a soup. They are much more fattening than rice, as they are made of wheat. Rice noodles are lighter, and a recipe for preparing rice noodles is included here.

It is a Chinese custom to serve noodles at birthdays. They are called "longevity noodles" on these occasions, and as the length of life is compared to the length of the noodles, it is very bad luck to cut the noodles or to break them during cooking and eating.

30 MINUTES
COOKING TIME

PLAIN

WHITE RICE

INGREDIENTS:

2 cups raw, long-grain white rice (not converted)
3½ cups water

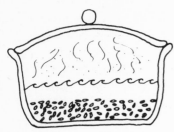

TO PREPARE:

1. Choose a pot which has 3—4" clearing on top after addition of rice and water. This space is for the steam which will finish cooking the rice.

2. Rinse the rice in running water until the water runs clear. This washes away the excess starch which will otherwise form a scum on the rice, giving the cooked rice a dirty gray surface.

3. Drain off all the rinsing water. Add 3½ cups water to the rice. The rice is now ready to cook.

TO COOK: *(cooking time about 30 minutes)*

1. Set the pot uncovered on a medium-high flame and bring mixture to a rapid boil.

2. Continue boiling, uncovered, for about 5 minutes until most of the water disappears and "fish eyes" or soap-like bubbles appear on the surface of the rice.

3. Cover the pot tightly, adjust the flame to lowest, and cook undisturbed for 20 minutes.

4. Turn off heat. Serve at once, or rice can keep warm in covered pot for up to one-half hour before serving.

5. To serve: Fluff up rice before ladling it into rice bowls.

6. Yield: Serves 4—6 people.

Notes: The Chinese never measure the portions of rice and water. Practice has perfected the art of cooking rice. I can tell the correct measures of water needed just by looking at the rice in the pot. Or, to play it safe, I rest my palm flat on top of the rice: the water level should come up to the wrist and cover the palm. You can also buy special electric steamers for cooking rice which have complete instructions for cooking different varieties of rice with them.

Keep left-over rice in a covered container in the refrigerator for 2—3 days. Reheat by steaming (see page 2 for steaming directions); or use it cold in fried rice dishes.

30 MINUTES
COOKING TIME

MINCED BEEF

RICE

INGREDIENTS:

2 cups white, long-grained rice (not converted)

—

2 medium onions, chopped coarsely
2 cloves garlic, chopped fine
3 tablespoons peanut or vegetable oil

—

1 lb. ground beef

—

Master sauce:
4 tablespoons dark soy
1 tablespoon cornstarch dissolved in ½ cup water
1 tablespoon Chinese rice wine or sherry
2 teaspoons sugar
1 teaspoon salt

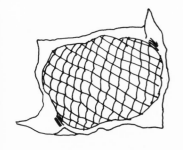

TO PREPARE:

1. Prepare rice by washing and draining according to directions on page 134.
2. Chop onions and garlic.
3. Make master sauce by combining all the ingredients in a cup.

TO COOK: (cooking time about 30 minutes)

1. Cook rice according to directions on page 134. Keep warm and proceed to make minced beef.
2. Heat 3 tablespoons oil in wok over high flame. Add onion and garlic and sizzle 3 minutes.
3. Add ground beef and stir-fry sizzling 2 minutes. Break up any lumps.
4. Add master sauce and cook stirring 1 minute for sauce to simmer and thicken. Serve.
5. To serve: Put the hot rice on a large platter, pour the beef on top and serve hot.
6. Yield: Serves 4.

Notes: This is a meal by itself. Chinese restaurants serve this as a quick meal, or as a popular lunch dish. Sometimes a raw or fried egg is served perched on top of each individual portion.

2 HOURS
COOKING TIME

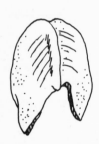

CHICKEN

CONGEE

INGREDIENTS:

>½ cup long-grained white rice (not converted)
>8 cups water
>—
>2 whole chicken breasts
>—
>1 tablespoon peanut or vegetable oil
>4 scallions, cut into ⅛" rings
>2 tablespoons light soy
>salt to taste

TO PREPARE:

1. Rinse and drain rice.
2. Wash chicken breasts and pat dry.
3. Cut scallions into ⅛" rings.

TO COOK: (cooking time about 2 hours)

1. Place the rice in a large heavy pot, add 8 cups water and bring to a boil uncovered.

2. Add chicken breasts, lower flame, cover pot and simmer 1½ hours. Stir every ½ hour to prevent sticking.

3. Lift out chicken breasts, discard bone, and shred the meat with fingers to thin strips.

4. Return meat to the congee and continue to simmer 15 minutes.

5. Add oil, scallions, light soy, and salt to taste. Stir to mix. Serve.

6. To serve: Serve hot in individual bowls. The congee can be cooked hours before and reheated.

7. Yield: Serves 4—6 people as brunch or light snack.

Notes: Congee, or "joke," is basically a thick rice soup. It is cooked like plain rice but with much more water. Prolonged cooking gives it a glutinous soupy consistency. In most parts of China, especially the cold North, breakfast and snacks consist of a large bowl of piping hot *congee*. Freshly made, smooth and glutinous *congee* requires about 2—3 hours of preparation. This means getting up before dawn to prepare, which is why *congee* nowadays is usually a Sunday brunch item to be eaten at leisure. A very simple *congee* can be leftover rice with boiling water poured over it, eaten with pickled turnips, fermented beancurds or dried ground meat. Then there's the quick *congee* which is cooked in one-half hour, with bits of chopped meat or leftover meat thrown in as seasoning. A really good *congee* simmers for hours, has elaborate flavoring like chicken and abalone, livers and kidneys, or seafood. The Chinese eat *congee* regularly for general well-being, for it is gentle and soothing to the system. Some people swear it's the best cure for a hangover. In China, *congee* stalls line the streets and are open all through the night.

10 MINUTES
COOKING TIME

PLAIN

NOODLES

INGREDIENTS:

> 6 ozs. dry noodles
> 8 cups water

TO COOK: *(cooking time about 10 minutes)*

1. Bring to boil 8 cups of water in a large pot.

2. Keep the water boiling, add the noodles, cook, stirring for 5 minutes. Drain and keep warm while you prepare sauce, soup, or meat dishes to go with it.

3. Yield: Serves 2.

Notes: There are two basic kinds of Chinese dry noodles. There are the yellow cakes of wheat noodles, which are referred to as "egg noodles" because of the eggs used in preparing their dough. These are sold in the form of woven balls, with 6–8 balls per bag. Drop the balls whole into boiling water and stir to unwind them as they are cooking. The second kind is the rice noodle. They are made from ground white rice. These noodles are very thin and are packed in one block in a bag. Break off the amount you need in cooking.

Please distinguish between the two kinds. Egg noodles are heavy and need strong seasoning while rice noodles are thinner, lighter, and are less heavy and fattening.

10 MINUTES
COOKING TIME

NOODLES IN CHICKEN BROTH

WITH HAM AND LETTUCE

INGREDIENTS:

6 ozs. dry egg noodles
8 cups water
—

one 12-oz. can clear chicken broth
1 can water
2 scallions, cut into 2" lengths
—

4 thin slices cooked ham, cut into strips
1 small lettuce, cut into strips
—

salt and white pepper to taste

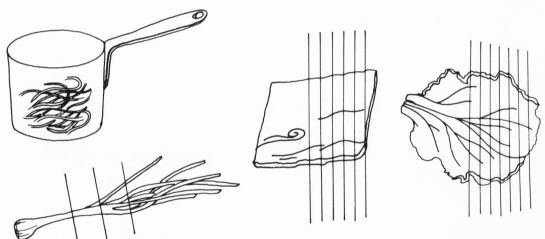

TO PREPARE:

1. Cook noodles according to the directions on page 138. Drain and keep warm.

2. Cut scallions into 2" pieces.

3. Cut ham into 2" x ½" strips.

4. Wash and separate stalks of lettuce. Cut crosswise into ½" strips.

TO COOK: *(cooking time about 10 minutes)*

1. Bring chicken broth, water, and scallions to boil in a pot.

2. Add ham and lettuce and boil uncovered 1 minute. Season soup with salt and white pepper.

3. To serve: Divide warm noodles in 2 large bowls. Pour soup over them, arrange ham and lettuce on top and serve hot.

4. Yield: Serves 2.

Notes: This is a quick meal with everything included in one bowl. You can use other soups from the soup section—choose the kinds which are quickly boiled, with meat and vegetables in them, rather than the thick and spicy ones.

NOODLES LO MIEN

WITH OYSTER SAUCE

10 MINUTES
COOKING TIME

INGREDIENTS:

6 ozs. dry egg noodles
8 cups water
—

Lo Mien *sauce:*
½ cup oyster sauce
3 tablespoons peanut or vegetable oil
6 pieces scallions, chopped fine
2 tablespoons fresh ginger, chopped fine
salt to taste

TO PREPARE:

1. Cook noodles according to directions on page 138.
2. Chop scallions and ginger finely. Make *Lo Mien* sauce by combining all the ingredients in a cup.

To serve: Place noodles in a large bowl and add the *Lo Mien* sauce, toss to mix. Serve warm.

Yield: Serves 2.

Notes: This is a very popular snack dish in China. It is tasty, and can be made in a jiffy, with very little cooking involved. Another sauce to go with this might be the bottled hot brown bean sauce with bits of light soy and sesame oil. *"Lo Mien"* means tossed noodles with seasonings.

NOODLES WITH STIR-FRIED GROUND BEEF

IN HOISIN SAUCE

INGREDIENTS:

6 ozs. dry egg noodles
8 cups water
—

½ lb. ground beef
2 tablespoons peanut or vegetable oil
2 cloves garlic, crushed coarsely
—

Master sauce:
3 tablespoons hoisin sauce
2 tablespoons dark soy
1 teaspoon cornstarch dissolved in ¼ cup water
¼ teaspoon salt

TO PREPARE:

1. Cook noodles according to directions on page 138. Drain and keep warm.

2. Crush garlic.

3. Make master sauce by combining all the ingredients in a cup.

TO COOK: (cooking time about 15 minutes)

1. Heat 3 tablespoons oil in wok over medium flame. Add garlic and sizzle ½ minute.

2. Add beef and stir-fry 2 minutes.

3. Add master sauce and cook stirring 1 minute for sauce to simmer and thicken.

4. To serve: Place warm noodles in a large bowl and pour beef and sauce over them. Serve hot at once.

5. Yield: Serves 2.

Notes: This is a very popular way of serving noodles in Shanghai. For a more spicy meal, use chopped scallions and leeks as a side dish, and pass red chili oil or hot brown bean sauce separately.

ADDITIONAL RECIPES:

Fried Rice with Ham, Eggs, and Scallions, see page 167

Cold Rice Noodles with Stir-Fried Beansprouts, see page 170

Menus and Suggestions for Entertaining Chinese Style

INTRODUCTION

In this chapter, I have prepared two types of menus. For one menu, you will find all you need in your local supermarket; the other will require shopping in a Chinese grocery store. Suggestions for serving cocktail canapes, wine, tea, and table setting arrangements are also given, and I have included a 5-finger game which is often played at the table during large dinner parties. The game is not unlike our stone—paper—scissors games in timing and guessing. It is really an excuse for drinking wine and it brings a sense of conviviality to the dinner table.

A balanced dinner includes meat, fish, and fresh vegetables. It should appeal to the sense of smell, taste, texture, and color. It should be a sampling of the different textures of food; crunchy green and white vegetables; crisp cooked shrimps; smooth, tender, black mushrooms; velvety chicken or fish. The natural consistency of each food is maintained and enhanced by the techniques of stir-frying, braising, and steaming and, of course, by the various sauces in which they are cooked.

When you plan a menu, keep in mind that stir-fry dishes require last minute cooking, so include only one or two in the menu. The other dishes in the menu might be a braised dish, a cold dish or a steamed dish which can be prepared in advance.

Both types of menus call for Chinese sauces and Chinese dry ingredients. By now you should have these stored in your kitchen cabinets. The supermarket menu includes meats, fish, and vegetables readily available in supermarkets. The Chinese grocery menu uses fresh beancurd, beansprouts, *bok choy,* snow peas, roast pork, or pickled turnip heads, most of which usually cannot be stored for more than a day or so. For most people, then, using the "Chinese grocery" menu will mean a special shopping trip unless they live near a Chinese community.

SUPERMARKET MENUS FOR FOUR TO SIX PERSONS

(1) Steamed chicken breasts with Chinese mushrooms
Stir-fried flank steaks in oyster sauce
Cucumber and celery salad
Plain rice

(2) Steamed ground beef with chopped scallions
Shallow-fried shrimps in ketchup sauce
Braised whole cucumbers with Chinese mushrooms
Plain rice

(3) Creamed corn egg-drop soup
Stir-fried ground beef and chopped smoked oysters
Stir-fried fresh broccoli in light soy
Plain rice

Real Chinese ingredients used are light and dark soy, Chinese mushrooms, fresh ginger, oyster sauce, and sesame oil.

CHINESE GROCERY STORE MENUS FOR FOUR TO SIX PERSONS

(1) Cold chicken breasts Trent
Braised pork lion heads with Chinese celery cabbage
Stir-fried beancurd in hot brown bean sauce
Plain rice

(2) Braised apricot-flavored duck in *hoisin* sauce
Stir-fried beancurd in oyster sauce
Stir-fried snow peas with celery and scallions
Plain rice

(3) Diced winter melon soup with small shrimps
Steamed pork slices with pickled kohlrabi heads
Stir-fried clams in *hoisin* sauce
Stir-fried monk-style vegetarian dish
Plain rice

Finally, here is a Szechuan menu for a very garlicky and spicy evening of dining—

(4) Braised eggplants with dried shrimps
     Stir-fried shrimps Szechuan in hot brown bean sauce
     Stir-fried diced chicken breasts in *hoisin* sauce
     Steamed lean pork served cold Szechuan style
     Plain rice

CHINESE COCKTAIL CANAPES

Begin your Chinese dinner with an offering of Chinese tidbits or appetizers with cocktails. Oriental or gourmet food shops sell cans of abalone, octopus, smoked oysters, and soy-sauce mushrooms. (If the large department stores in your area do not have gourmet food sections, consult the Yellow Pages of your telephone directory.) Cut the abalone and octopus into bite-sized pieces and arrange with the other foods on a tray. Provide tiny bamboo spears or toothpicks.

If you are shopping in Chinatown the night of your dinner, get some ready made *dim sums*—small dumplings available in tea shops or cafes that can be bought to take out. Reheat and serve to your guests for a special treat.

TABLE SETTING FOR A SIT-DOWN DINNER

Chinese households usually have a round table so that the main dishes are within easy reach of everyone. If you have a rectangular table, you will probably not entertain more than six to eight guests to a sit-down dinner. Everyone should be able to reach all of the dishes easily, for Chinese dishes are not supposed to be lifted and passed around. Eight guests or more can be accommodated if two servings of every dish are available, but for less work and fewer dishes, buffet-style dinners are best for larger groups.

For the sit-down dinner, each setting should include:

      A pair of chopsticks
      A porcelain spoon for soup and sauces
      A tiny saucer for resting the spoon, or for soy sauce
      A rice bowl and its saucer which doubles as bone plate.
      A small cup for tea or wine

These are the basic pieces. You may need extra bowls and cups for soup tea, and wines; it depends on what you will serve.

When the dinner is ready, bring all the dishes to the table at the same time. (An elaborate banquet with more than ten dishes and extra help is a different matter altogether.) When the guests are seated, everyone begins by dipping his chopsticks or spoon into the dishes and taking whatever he wants. Do not lift the plates and pass around to serve individual portions; just hold your chopsticks, determine which morsel you would like and remove it to your bowl. Raking the dish for a buried piece is considered very bad manners. An expert, of course, can extricate a buried piece of food with a flash of the chopsticks and it is not considered raking. *Yum Sing!* 飲 勝 (Bottoms Up!)

A BUFFET-STYLE DINNER

A buffet-style dinner is very simple to serve; you don't even need to have rice bowls. All you need is a stack of plates and forks and serving spoons for the rice and other dishes. Each guest helps himself by piling what he likes onto his plate and eating it from there.

If, however, you provide chopsticks for a buffet-style dinner, you must also provide a spoon. In China, plate meals (as from a quick-order restaurant) are eaten with a porcelain spoon and a pair of chopsticks, and it is the spoon that carries most of the food to the mouth. The chopsticks are only used for the graceful selection of morsels of meat or vegetable, never for picking up the rice itself when eating from a plate.

WINE

There is a Chinese table wine which is served warm throughout the meal in China. It is light brown in color, made from wheat, and tastes like warm sherry. This yellow wine, *Wong Jowl* or *Shao Shing,* is 28 proof and is sold in Chinese liquor stores. Perhaps next time you will serve this to your guests. If not, dry white wines go well with Chinese food. In Hong Kong, many people serve a chilled Moselle wine for its delicate bouquet.

5-FINGERS GAME

With food and wine on the table, what is lacking in a Chinese dinner? Noise! Here's where the fingers game comes in. How to play? The game rules are simple: using one hand each, two or three players stick out any number of fingers and, at the same time, guess and call out loud the total number of fingers that will show in the group. The one who guesses the right number of fingers wins. The loser is penalized by having to take sips of wine. Very often, though, the winner shows he is a sport by drinking along with the loser.

TEA CHA

Tea or *cha* can be sipped throughout the meal if you're not serving wine. Otherwise serve a nice pot of hot, fragrant Chinese tea to signify the end of the meal. Desserts are rare and seldom served, though fresh fruit in season is a regular treat for the family at the end of each meal. The Chinese believe fruits help digestion and give a feeling of well being.

If you don't have a favorite brand of Chinese tea yet, spend some time now tasting the popular brands, then settle for your favorite and take pride in serving it often. It's like choosing a perfume or wine, an essential part of the art of civilized living.

Every time I remember a special place (visits to my grandmother, my aunts, or to a friend's home), the aroma of different but particular kinds of tea comes to my mind. When I first knew my husband, Peter, he told me that the tea that my sister-in-law served was exceptional, and couldn't we have some like it. Now, every time he has that tea, he never fails to remember her.

Chinese tea is always brewed fresh in boiling water just before serving. After five to ten minutes of steeping, it is poured and sipped while still very hot. It is drunk plain, without milk or sugar. Tea leaves in the cup are very common, but a tea strainer, milk, and sugar are not!

For simple classification, tea can be divided into three groups:

Green Tea   A pale green brew with a delicate flavor which has a cooling effect on the body. Well known brands are Dragon Well and Water Nymph.

Dark Tea   The brew is dark brown and the taste robust. It is good for the digestion, especially after a heavy meal. Some brands are Iron Kwan Yin, Keemun and Look On.

Scented Tea   This is essentially a mixture of green tea with flower petals. The brew is pale yellow-green, very aromatic, and the taste is fragrant and permeating. It has a great soothing and relaxing influence. This kind of tea is a very appropriate choice for the end of a Chinese dinner and to sip well into the night when the last guest leaves. Among these are jasmine tea, water nymph with narcissus, chrysanthemum tea and rose tea.

The Three Great Dinners: A Vegetarian Dinner

VEGETARIAN FOOD: *YIN* AND *YANG*

The Chinese love eating vegetables. They believe vegetables improve their health and prolong their lives. Meat is thought to be the cause of all sorts of ailments from indigestion to high blood pressure. Also, the Buddhist religion, which was widespread in China, forbade its monks to eat meat, and required its followers to abstain from it on the first and fifteenth day of the month. In addition, the more fervent followers abstained from meat one month each year.

To make meatless meals interesting, very elaborate vegetarian dishes were created by Buddhist monks in the monastery kitchens. As these kitchens also had to serve meals to the worshipping public when they came to buy altar incense and oil for the gods, it was important that the food was first rate. Vegetables grown in the monastery gardens with natural (!) saintly fertilizer were disguised in different shapes and sauces to produce the now world famous *Nine Big Dishes Monk's Cuisine,* the set of nine dishes traditionally served at a Buddhist meal. The nine dishes have names like meatless roast duck, chicken, fried shrimps. The look and texture are achieved by shaping vegetables and bending beancurds and adding dazzling sauces to deceive the eyes.

The unusually good health and long lives of Buddhist monks have been attributed to the carefully prepared vegetable diet they follow. This art of preparing balanced, nutritious food to build long lives and alert minds is now referred to as "macrobiotics" (great vitality or life). In Chinese practice, macrobiotics is the careful blending of the two opposite elements of the principle of life: the *Yin* and the *Yang*. The ideal balance of *Yin* and *Yang* is 5 to 1; when life is in perfect order, harmony, health and happiness result. To apply *Yin* and *Yang* to the food we eat, let's take a look at their properties:

Yin is female; earth, cold, darkness. In food, it's the vegetables, the sugar, the acid, the potassium.

Yang is male; strength, light, warmth. In food, it's the meat, the salt, the alkali, the sodium.

Some of the *Yin* foods are: beansprouts, broccoli, eggplant, melon, mushrooms, spinach, cucumber, soybeans, garlic, celery, peanut oil, green pepper, beancurd, lettuce, bamboo shoots, wine.

Some of the *Yang* foods are meat, shrimps, fish, watercress, carrots, onions, rice, apples, chestnuts, tea, coffee, salt, Chinese cabbage, ginger, eggs, milk.

At first glance, it seems that there are too many *Yin* foods to choose from and not enough *Yang* foods to achieve the 5 to 1 ratio. Not quite. All food can be made, for example, more *Yang* through varying the qualities of heat, salt, pressure, and time. (Is it locally grown, has it been stored long?) Also, each individual's body chemistry or reaction to food is different. Some people are basically very *Yang* or *Yin* to begin with. So it's through trial-and-error and knowing yourself that you'll find your own balance.

What are the symptoms when you're not having a balanced *Yin-Yang*, 5-to-1 diet? Well, too much *Yin* (or sugar or acid) causes cramps, itching, and pimples. Signs that the body is expelling the excess *Yin* may be found in sneezing, coughing, hiccuping, blinking, or watering of the eyes. Too much *Yang* (or salt or alkali) causes indigestion, bad breath, and constipation. Meat causes body odor, especially under the arms, and dandruff. Meat eaters are more temperamental and explosive than the quiet vegetable eaters. You are what you eat!

Some may think it impossible and confusing to balance or observe their *Yin* and *Yang*. Chinese families practice it naturally, with no fuss or anxiety; the balance of the two elements and their instinctive differentiation is instilled through old wives' tales, the "do's" and "don'ts" handed down from the elders. Just as you would take an alkali medication (*Yang*) to soothe an acidic stomach (*Yin*) when too many *Yin* symptoms manifest themselves, steps are taken to counterbalance it by a change of diet to the *Yang*. That's when all the herb teas and medicinal brews are used. One or two cups administered correctly will bring you back in equilibrium again.

The Buddhists' belief that you are what you eat extends beyond the selection of food to its preparation and presentation. You should not only choose your food to have a good *Yin-Yang* balance, but you should relax and prepare it lovingly, so as not to impart your negative and uncharitable feelings to those who will eat it. Buddhist monks themselves enter the kitchen reverently, emptied of all earthly thoughts. Their food is prepared lovingly, respectfully, in a clean and uncluttered kitchen. Their tools are basic and natural, clay or earthen pots and wood for fuel. Finally, they believe, when it is eaten, food should be chewed slowly and savored, and harmony and peace will come.

As the love of vegetarian, macrobiotic, or natural food now seems to be as much a part of the Western scene as it is of the Eastern, soybeans and soy sauce have become the base of many natural food dishes here. I've assembled here four simple dishes so that you can give an elaborate Oriental vegetarian dinner to beguile your friends. The vegetables chosen are all readily available and the dishes taste completely different because of the use of various sauces.

Empty your mind, go back to nature while you dine on this rejuvenating food.

MENU FOR A VEGETARIAN DINNER
    Stir-fried monk-style vegetarian dish
    Stir-fried fresh broccoli in light soy
    Braised Chinese mushrooms and *bok choy* in dark soy
    Cucumber and celery salad
    Plain white rice
    Tea

**10 MINUTES
COOKING TIME**

STIR-FRIED MONK-STYLE

VEGETARIAN DISH

INGREDIENTS:

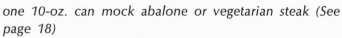

2 small bok choy, *slant-cut into 1" pieces*
2 thin slices fresh ginger
2 tablespoons peanut or vegetable oil

—

one 8-oz. can sliced bamboo shoots, drained
¼ lb. fresh snow pea pods, strings removed

—

one 10-oz. can mock abalone or vegetarian steak (See page 18)
6 Chinese mushrooms, soaked in water until soft
2 ozs. cellophane noodles, soaked in water until soft
2 tablespoons peanut or vegetable oil

—

Master sauce:
4 tablespoons oyster sauce
2 tablespoons dark soy
1 teaspoon cornstarch dissolved in ½ cup water
1 tablespoon sesame oil

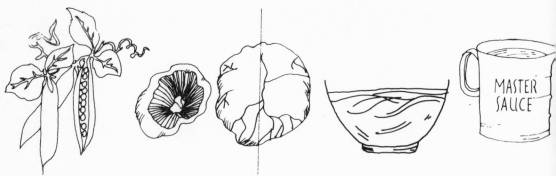

TO PREPARE:

1. Separate *bok choy* stalks, wash and drain, slant-cut into 1" pieces.
2. Cut 2 thin slices fresh ginger.
3. Remove strings from snow pea pods.
4. Discard stems of softened mushrooms. Halve.
5. Cover cellophane noodles with water, soak until soft.
6. Make master sauce by combining all the ingredients in a cup.

TO COOK: *(cooking time about 10 minutes)*

1. Heat 2 tablespoons of oil in wok over medium flame. Add ginger and sizzle ½ minute.

2. Add *bok choy* and stir-fry 2 minutes.

3. Add bamboo shoots and snow pea pods and stir-fry 1 minute. Transfer to a plate.

4. Heat 2 tablespoons of oil in the same wok over medium flame. Add mock abalone, mushrooms, and cellophane noodles, stir-fry ½ minute.

5. Keep mixture at a simmer, add master sauce and cook stirring ½ minute till mixture simmers and thickens.

6. Add the cooked vegetables from plate and stir to mix. It is now ready to serve.

7. To serve: Dish up in a large platter and serve hot. This dish can sit in a warm oven for 10 minutes.

8. Yield: Serves 6 in a 4-course dinner.

Notes: Other vegetables that can be substituted for *bok choy* or snow peas are: celery, cucumber, or carrot slices. Mock abalone or vegetable steaks can be omitted if not available.

Oyster sauce is acceptable in a vegetarian diet because a devout monk was once told that anything that clung to his staff when plunged into the water could be part of his vegetable diet. Oysters were found clinging to his staff and so they are acceptable.

5 MINUTES
COOKING TIME

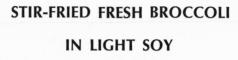

STIR-FRIED FRESH BROCCOLI

IN LIGHT SOY

INGREDIENTS:

    2 medium bunches broccoli
    2 tablespoons peanut or vegetable oil
    2 thin slices fresh ginger

    —

    Sauce A:
    1 teaspoon Chinese rice wine or sherry
    ½ teaspoon salt
    ½ teaspoon sugar
    ¼ cup water

    —

    Sauce B:
    1 tablespoon light soy
    1 teaspoon cornstarch dissolved in 1 tablespoon water

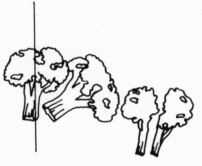
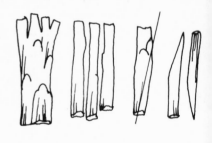

TO PREPARE:

    1. Wash broccoli and cut each bunch into 2 parts: the flower part and the stem part. Cut each flower part lengthwise into small pieces so that each piece is a cluster of stems and flowers. Peel tough skin of stem apart. Quarter the stem lengthwise, then slant-cut quartered stem into 2″ x 1″ pieces.

    2. Cut 2 thin slices fresh ginger.

    3. Make sauce A and B in 2 separate cups. Set aside.

TO COOK: *(cooking time about 5 minutes)*

1. Heat 2 tablespoons oil in wok over medium flame. Add 2 thin slices ginger, sizzle ½ minute.

2. Add broccoli pieces, stir-fry 2 minutes.

3. Add sauce A, stir, cover wok, and sizzle 1 minute.

4. Remove cover, keep mixture simmering, add sauce B and cook stirring ½ minute till sauce simmers and thickens. Serve.

5. To serve: Dish up and serve hot at once, to savor the crunchy broccoli. It cannot be reheated or left to sit.

6. Yield: Serves 6 in a 4-course dinner.

Notes: Almost all other fresh Chinese vegetables, especially the green ones, can be cooked this way. Try using *bok choy,* mustard green, beansprouts, cucumber slices or spinach like this.

35 MINUTES
COOKING TIME

BRAISED CHINESE MUSHROOMS

AND BOK CHOY IN DARK SOY

INGREDIENTS:

3 tablespoons peanut or vegetable oil
2 thin slices fresh ginger
—

12 large Chinese mushrooms soaked in water until soft
¼ cup dark soy
1 teaspoon sugar
1 teaspoon Chinese rice wine or sherry

2 small bok choy, slant-cut into 2" pieces
½ cup water
¼ teaspoon salt
—

1 tablespoon cornstarch dissolved in 1 tablespoon water

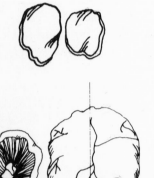

TO PREPARE:

1. Cut 2 thin slices fresh ginger.
2. Discard stems of softened mushrooms.
3. Separate stalks of *bok choy*, wash and drain. Slant-cut into 2" pieces.
4. Make cornstarch solution and set aside.

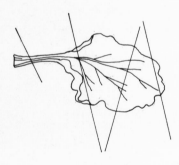

TO COOK: *(cooking time about 35 minutes)*

1. Heat 3 tablespoons oil in a heavy casserole over medium flame. Add ginger and sizzle ½ minute.
2. Add mushrooms, dark soy, sugar, and wine. Cover and simmer 15 minutes.
3. Add *bok choy*, water and salt. Bring to a boil uncovered. Cover pot, lower flame and simmer 15 minutes.
4. Keep mixture simmering, add cornstarch solution, and cook stirring ½ minute for sauce to simmer and thicken. Serve.
5. To serve: Serve very hot in the casserole. This dish can sit for ½ hour, and can be gently reheated to be served hot.
6. Yield: Serves 6 in a 4-course dinner.
Notes: This is a very popular vegetable dish and is served often at a vegetarian dinner.

CUCUMBER AND CELERY

SALAD

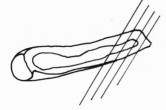

INGREDIENTS:

    2 cucumbers, peeled, halved, seeds removed
    1 teaspoon salt

    —

    1 whole celery, strings removed and peeled
    2 scallions, cut into 2" pieces

    —

    Chinese salad dressing:
    2 tablespoons light soy
    3 tablespoons sesame oil
    2 tablespoons peanut or vegetable oil
    3 tablespoons white vinegar
    2 tablespoons sugar
    salt to taste

TO PREPARE:

    1. Peel and halve cucumbers. Scoop out and discard seeds. Cut into ⅛" slices. Put in a bowl, sprinkle with salt, and let sit for ½ hour. Drain off collected liquid.

    2. Remove strings from celery stalks. Peel tough outside skin. Cut stalks into 2" lengths, then cut into 2 x ¼" strips.

    3. Cut scallions into 2" strips.

    4. Make Chinese salad dressing by combining all the ingredients in a cup.

TO MAKE:

    1. In a large salad bowl mix together drained cucumber slices, celery strips, and scallions.

    2. Add the Chinese salad dressing and toss well to mix.

    3. Cover and chill for ½–1 hour. Serve cold.

    4. Yield: Serves 6 in a 4-course dinner.

    Notes: Vary amounts of vinegar and sugar to taste. A very interesting addition to this salad is skinned raw peanuts. Cook peanuts in boiling water for 15 minutes. Drain and cool, salt to taste, and add to salad.

The Three
Great Dinners:
A Winter
Feast

THE FIRE POT

On cold winter nights, the Chinese keep warm by having a fire-pot or hot-pot dinner. The food is cooked on the table in a pot of boiling broth over a small charcoal fire. The "proper" fire pot available in Chinatown has space for the broth as well as little wire strainers in which to cook the food, and room under the pot for the charcoal. You can substitute an electric casserole, a fondue casserole, or just a pot on a burner. THE POT OF BROTH MUST BE KEPT BOILING CONSTANTLY THROUGHOUT THE MEAL to cook the pieces of meat or vegetables dipped in it. Wooden chopsticks or forks with wooden handles (which don't conduct the heat) are ideal for cooking the food.

There are a variety of fire pots; namely, the Chrysanthemum fire pot, the Mongolian fire pot, the Ten-Variety fire pot, and a Combination Family-Style fire pot. Whatever the name, they all use the same basic fondue-cooking principles—a pot of boiling broth over constant heat, and ingredients sliced thinly or cut into bite-sized pieces ready to be cooked. At the dinner table, each guest dunks the food briefly into the boiling broth, one morsel at a time. His cooked piece is then dipped into his own bowl of sauce and eaten while hot. At the end of the meal, the rich soup that is now in the pot is served in bowls to the guests.

The difference between the various fire pots is in the choice of ingredients. The Chrysanthemum pot has the most variety; chicken, beef and liver, fish, shrimps, oysters and squids, as well as lettuce, spinach, Chinese celery and cabbage, plus cellophane noodles and beancurd are all used. The dipping sauce is made of raw eggs (to soothe and cool), soy, wine, and sesame oil.

The Mongolian pot uses only lamb and no seafood. The vegetables and other ingredients are similar to those used in the Chrysanthemum pot. The dipping sauce, however, has spicy condiments added to it such as chopped scallions, garlic, ginger, Chinese parsley, vinegar, and hot chili oil.

The Ten-Variety pot consists mainly of pre-cooked foods such as ham, shrimp balls, beef slices, and vegetables arranged neatly in the hot broth and brought to the table to be served at once.

My favorite is the recipe below—the Wong's Family-Style fire pot served by my mother.

A fire-pot dinner is definitely winter fare because of the heat of cooking round a fire and from the bubbling broth. The food cooked in this way is considered very "heating" and "dry" to the body. As this combination may lead to nose bleeds, sore throats, and thirst, it is necessary to drink plenty of water and broth after a fire-pot dinner.

WONG'S FAMILY-STYLE

FIRE-POT DINNER

INGREDIENTS:

> 1 lb. flank steak, cut into ⅛" slices
> 2 whole chicken breasts, skinned and boned and sliced
>   ⅛" thick
> ½ lb. calf liver, sliced ⅛" thick
> —
> 1 lb. small raw shrimps, shelled
> 1 lb. fillet of sole or flounder, sliced ⅛" thick
> 4 fresh squid, cleaned, boned, and sliced into 1" pieces
> 1 dozen shucked fresh oysters or 2 dozen clams
> —
> ½ lb. fresh spinach
> 1 lb. lettuce
> —
> 4 ozs. cellophane noodles, soaked in water until soft
> 6 pieces fresh beancurd, quartered
> —
> two 12-oz. cans clear chicken broth
> 6 cups water
> —
> Master sauce:
> 2 cups dark soy
> 3 tablespoons Chinese rice wine or sherry
> ¼ cup sesame oil
> 3 tablespoons sugar
> salt to taste
> —
> Optional extras for sauce:*
> ½ cup vinegar
> ½ cup red chili oil
> ½ cup finely chopped scallions
> ½ cup finely chopped ginger
> ¼ cup finely chopped garlic

* Each guest takes ¼ cup master sauce and then adds extra spices to taste.

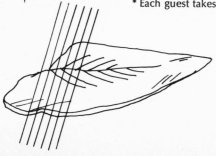

TO PREPARE:

1. Halve the flank steak lengthwise, then cut crosswise into ⅛" slices.

2. Bone and skin chicken breasts, slice ⅛" thick.

3. Slice calf's liver ⅛" thick.

4. Shell shrimps.

5. Slice fish ⅛" thick.

6. Clean squids, cut into 1" pieces.

7. Use the oysters and clams *whole*.

8. Arrange cut meat attractively on 2 large plates, each having equal portions of beef, chicken and liver. Do the same for the seafood. Cover and chill.

9. Wash spinach and lettuce, drain and cut into 2" pieces. Put in a large bowl and chill.

10. Cover cellophane noodles in water and soak till soft, put on a plate, cover and chill.

11. Quarter beancurd, put on a plate, cover and chill.

12. Master sauce: Combine dark soy, wine, sesame oil, sugar, and salt in a large bowl. This is the basic sauce and allows ¼ cup for each guest.

Chop the garlic, scallions, and ginger and put all the ingredients in separate small bowls for guests to add to their basic sauce as they prefer.

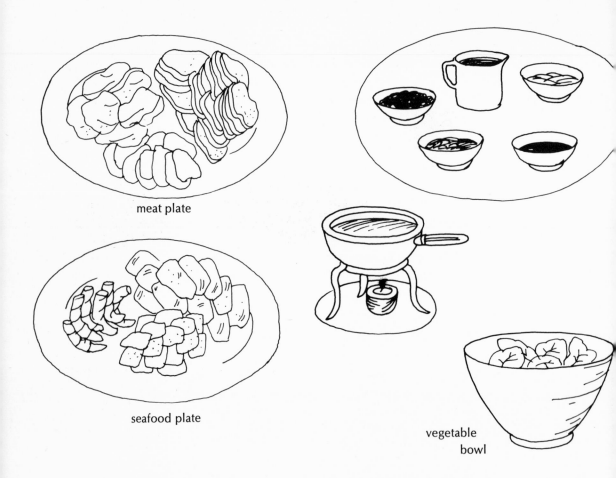

meat plate

seafood plate

vegetable
bowl

TO COOK:

1. Bring chicken broth and water to boil in a large pot. Bring broth to dining table in the pot and keep it boiling on charcoal burner or electric ring, etc.

2. Surround the fire pot with the plates of meat, seafood, vegetables, cellophane noodles, and beancurd.

3. Before sitting down to cook, each guest makes ¼ cup of the dipping sauce from the sauce tray.

4. Start cooking with the meat and seafood first. Everyone cooks by taking a morsel of food in his chopsticks (or speared on a fork) and dipping it into the boiling broth until cooked to his liking. (Take care not to lose your morsel in all this activity!)

5. Dip the cooked morsel into your own master sauce and eat while hot. Repeat until all the meat and seafood are eaten. You will need to add water (or stock) if the broth has been too reduced by boiling.

6. Add the remaining vegetables, beancurd, and cellophane noodles to the pot. Cover, bring to a boil, and cook for one minute. Serve the soup in individual bowls, include bits of everything in each serving. Delicious.

7. Yield: Serves 6—8. This is a meal in itself since a variety of ingredients are involved. There's a fair amount of cutting to be done beforehand, but the host does not have to do any cooking except his own. Isn't this a lovely way to spend a cold winter evening? Serve lots of wine with this meal, as the Chinese believe it's compulsory with a fire-pot dinner to help digestion and to kill any germs that survive the fire-pot dunking.

The Three Great Dinners: A Summer Feast

LETTUCE LOAVES AND COLD NOODLES

In the heat of the summer, the Chinese indulge in a rare cold meal which normally is considered too "cool" for the body system. The center of this cold dinner is *sun choy bow* 生菜包 which means "wrapped fresh lettuce leaves." For this you'll need lettuce leaves, fried rice and stir-fried ground beef with chopped smoked oysters, plus *hoisin* sauce for seasoning. Each guest takes a lettuce leaf, spreads *hoisin* sauce on the inside, spoons fried rice and ground meat into it, wraps the leaf up loosely, and picks up the "loaf" with his fingers. He then bites into a delicious combination of crisp lettuce, tangy *hoisin* sauce, tasty meat, and fried-rice filling.

Beginners in the art of eating lettuce loaves must remember that the loaf should be small, about 2" x 3", so that the leaves can be folded loosely without spilling the goodies inside. Still, two or three loaves may be all you want to tackle. For this reason, cold rice noodles, tossed with beansprouts, are included to provide a great summer feast.

The menu and directions for preparing and serving will be given first. The actual recipes follow at the end of this section.

THE MENU

Lettuce loaves filled with fried rice and ground beef and oysters
Cold rice noodles with beansprouts and roast pork

PREPARING THE FOOD

For the *lettuce loaves* you will need:

24 fresh lettuce leaves
Fried rice with ham, eggs, and scallions
Stir-fried ground beef with chopped smoked oysters
1 cup of *hoisin* sauce (see page 15)

lettuce

beef

fried rice

hoisin
sauce

cold noodles

rice bowl

None of the dishes is served hot. You start cooking early and just leave the dishes out on the table. *Do not refrigerate.*

Buy three large heads of iceberg lettuce. Wash and separate under tap water, taking care not to break the leaves. Shake off moisture, put in salad bowl and chill until dinner is ready.

Fry the rice two or three hours before dinner. Let sit in covered pot. Bring to the table in a large serving bowl when dinner is ready.

Cook the beef dish an hour before dinner. Put on a large platter till ready to serve.

Place one cup of *hoisin* sauce in a bowl.

Cook the *cold noodles* according to the recipe below, and serve the whole meal as follows:

SERVING THE FOOD

Group lettuce leaves, fried rice, ground beef dish and *hoisin* sauce in a circle on the table.

Each guest has a place setting of a dinner plate, a spoon, and a rice bowl for the fried rice.

Each guest puts a lettuce leaf on his plate, uses a small spoon to spread the *hoisin* sauce on the leaf, adds a spoonful of fried rice and a spoonful of beef, wraps it all up and eats.

Prepare and season the cold noodles dish ½ hour before dinner and arrange on one side of dining table. Serve noodles on plates after guests have finished with the lettuce loaves.

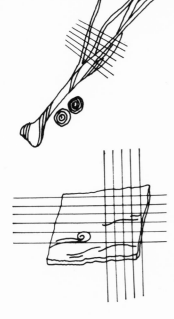

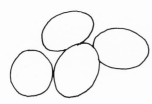

FRIED RICE WITH HAM,

EGGS, AND SCALLIONS

INGREDIENTS:

2 cups white long-grained rice (not converted)

—

3 tablespoons peanut or vegetable oil
6 scallions, cut into ⅛" rings

—

1 cup cooked ham, diced into ¼" cubes

—

4 eggs, lightly beaten

—

4 tablespoons light soy
salt to taste

TO PREPARE:

1. Cook the rice according to directions on page 134 half an hour before actual frying.
2. Cut scallions into ⅛" rings.
3. Dice ham into ¼" cubes.
4. Beat the eggs.

TO COOK: *(cooking time about 10 minutes)*

1. Use a large casserole or skillet which can hold all the cooked rice. In it heat 3 tablespoons oil over medium flame. Add scallions and stir-fry 1 minute.
2. Add diced ham and stir-fry 1 minute.
3. Pour the beaten eggs on top and cook undisturbed till eggs are half-set, about ½ minute.
4. Working quickly, use a wooden spoon to scrape all the cooked rice into the skillet. Stir-fry 2—3 minutes to mix thoroughly so that all the rice is coated with the eggs.
5. Add light soy and salt to taste. Stir to mix. Serve.
6. To serve: Serve hot at once, or, if used in lettuce loaves, allow to sit two to three hours in pot. Bring to the table in a large serving bowl when ready.
7. Yield: Serves 4—6 alone or 6—8 in a lettuce-loaves dinner.

Notes: This dish can also be served hot when used for a different kind of meal. It can be kept hot, covered, in the oven for one-half hour.

Roast pork or any left-over roast meat can be used instead of ham, if diced up and used the same way.

5 MINUTES
COOKING TIME

STIR-FRIED GROUND BEEF

AND CHOPPED SMOKED OYSTERS

INGREDIENTS:

1 lb. ground beef
2 tablespoons peanut or vegetable oil
2 cloves garlic

—

Master sauce:
2 teaspoons cornstarch dissolved in ¼ cup water
2 tablespoons dark soy
1 teaspoon Chinese rice wine or sherry
1 teaspoon sugar
½ teaspoon salt
white pepper to taste

—

one 4-oz. can smoked oysters

TO PREPARE:

1. Crush garlic.
2. Make master sauce by combining all the ingredients in a cup.
3. Drain oysters, chop coarsely.

TO COOK: *(cooking time about 5 minutes)*

1. Heat 2 tablespoons oil in wok over high flame. Add garlic and sizzle ½ minute.

2. Add ground beef and stir-fry sizzling 3 minutes. Keep breaking up any lumps.

3. Keep mixture at a simmer, add master sauce and cook stirring 1 minute for sauce to simmer and thicken.

4. Add chopped smoked oysters and stir-fry ½ minute to mix.

5. To serve: Serve hot at once, or, if used in lettuce loaves, cook an hour before dinner and put out on a large platter until ready to bring to the table.

6. Yield: Serves 2 alone, or 6 to 8 for a lettuce-loaves dinner.

Notes: This dish can also be served hot when included in a different type of dinner. If served hot, it can sit in a warm oven, covered, for 10 minutes. An attractive way of serving it is to line the plate with shredded fresh lettuce for color and crunch before piling the beef on top.

COLD RICE NOODLES

WITH STIR-FRIED BEANSPROUTS

NOODLES
INGREDIENTS:

> one ½-lb. packet rice noodles (not wheat noodles)
> 10 cups water
>
> —
>
> *Sauce for Noodles:*
> ½ cup white vinegar
> ½ cup light soy
> Tabasco sauce to taste
> salt to taste

TO COOK:

1. Bring water to boil in a large pot. Add rice noodles and boil 2 minutes. Cover pot, turn off heat, and cook 10 minutes. Drain noodles, rinse with cold water and drain again. Put in a large bowl.

2. Add vinegar, soy, salt, and Tabasco to taste. Toss to mix. Cover and chill till ready to serve. Serve with stir-fried beansprouts with roast pork (page 171).

5 MINUTES
COOKING TIME

STIR-FRIED BEANSPROUTS

WITH ROAST PORK

INGREDIENTS:

2 eggs lightly beaten

—

1 lb. fresh beansprouts, rinsed and drained
8 scallions, cut into 2" pieces
2 tablespoons peanut or vegetable oil
½ lb. roast pork, cut into 2" x ⅛" strips
10 Chinese mushrooms, soaked in water until soft
2 tablespoons peanut or vegetable oil

—

Master sauce:
¼ cup light soy
1 teaspoon cornstarch dissolved in 2 tablespoons water

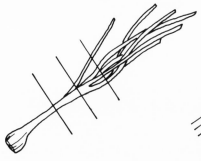

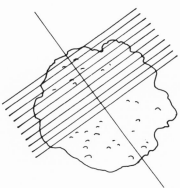

TO PREPARE:

1. Make a thin flat omelet with the 2 eggs. Transfer to a plate and cut into thin strips 2" x ⅛".

2. Cut scallions into 2" pieces.

3. Cut roast pork (or substitute cooked ham) into thin strips 2" x ⅛".

4. Discard stems and cut softened mushrooms into ⅛" strips.

5. Make master sauce in a cup.

TO COOK: *(cooking time about 5 minutes)*

1. Heat 2 tablespoons oil in wok over medium flame. Add scallions and beansprouts, stir-fry 1 minute. Transfer to a plate.

2. Heat 2 additional tablespoons oil in the same wok over medium flame. Add roast pork and mushrooms and stir-fry 1 minute.

3. Keep mixture simmering, add master sauce and cook stirring 1 minute for sauce to simmer and thicken.

4. Add the egg strips, cooked beansprouts, and scallions. Stir to mix ½ minute. Place on platter and serve hot at once, or, if used with cold rice noodles, cool to room temperature.

5. To serve: Place tossed, chilled noodles on a large platter. Top with the beansprout dish and serve.

6. Yield: Serves 6—8 persons as part of the lettuce-loaves feast.

Notes: Some people prefer not to toss the noodles in the sauce, but place the noodles, sauce, and beansprout dish all on separate platters and let the guests season the noodles themselves.

RECIPE INDEX

GENERAL INDEX